The Persian Shepherd Boy
and Other Tales

The Persian Shepherd Boy
and Other Tales

SERMON STORIES FOR THE MODERN ERA

ROBERT KARL GNUSE

WIPF *&* STOCK · Eugene, Oregon

THE PERSIAN SHEPHERD BOYS AND OTHER TALES
Sermon Stories for the Modern Era

Wipf & Stock
An Imprint of Wipf and Stock Publishers
199 W. 8th Ave., Suite 3
Eugene, OR 97401

www.wipfandstock.com

PAPERBACK ISBN: 979-8-3852-2244-5
HARDCOVER ISBN: 979-8-3852-2245-2
EBOOK ISBN: 979-8-3852-2246-9

VERSION NUMBER 05/16/24

CONTENTS

Preface | *vii*

HISTORICAL MEMORIES | **1**

The Little Persian Shepherd Boy | 1

A Doll Named Bippy | 5

The Lenten Goose | 11

Siberian Lutherans | 14

Elizabeth of Hungary | 17

Hans Walter Wolff's Story | 19

Silly Goose | 23

The Man Who Planted Trees | 24

FOLKLORE STORIES | **26**

The Small Puppy | 26

The Winter Field | 28

Little Birds in a Country Barn | 30

Dropped Books | 34

The Bishop's Choice | 35

The Fur Trappers | 37

The Cliff | 39

The Log | 41

Three Brick Masons | 43

The Admiral's Ship | 44

The Scratched Diamond | 46

The Rabbi's Journey | 48

Fables | 51

Nervous Angels | 51

The Rainman | 55

The Fourth Wise Man | 57

The Rabbi's Prayer | 61

The Fool on the Fence | 63

Killer Watermelons | 64

Spear in the Air | 67

Wine and the Country Doctor | 69

The Father's Palace | 70

Just Little Birds | 72

The Cracked Pot | 74

Rising Floodwaters | 76

PREFACE

I HAVE BEEN PREACHING sermons since 1970. Like many preachers, I know that a good story makes for a strong sermon. Sometimes the story is the only thing that people remember; sometimes it may be the only thing to which people listen closely during your sermon. Thus, I have always looked for good dramatic stories to tell; ones that people will remember and ones that carry a significant religious message by themselves. Many stories have passed through my lips over the past half century, but I believe the following selection of narratives constitute the best. I have looked for narratives with a specifically modern twist to them. I do not know how to define modern, but I think that it is material that speaks to people in a dramatic and fresh way. I was inspired to begin collecting these narratives after I began to list my own actual experiences and personal memories in the modern era, which I had effectively used as sermon stories.

I offer these narratives with parallel biblical passages that might go well with the accounts. I also offer some observations after the biblical text. These observations are short, for this is a book of sermon stories, not sermons.

I was inspired by a book entitled *Visit to Five Brothers and Other Double Exposures* by Ewald Bash (St. Louis: Concordia, 1968). I oft have used material from this book. I would include some of his accounts, but you can still purchase this wonderful little volume on Amazon. Like him, I recount a creative modern parable followed by a biblical passage. Unlike him, I dare to offer some theological insights. Hopefully, you may find my volume as helpful in sermonizing as I found his.

Historical Memories

THESE ARE ACTUAL MEMORIES of events that actually happened. Some of them were events in which I was personally involved and others were memories that were told to me by my father or a professor. To me these are the most dramatic stories because they happened. They also breathe the modern age. Sometimes life is more dramatic than fiction.

The Little Persian Shepherd Boy

High in the mountains of Persia a small isolated village survived with its simple lifestyle of farming and raising livestock. For them time stood still, unchanged over countless centuries. The village's flock of sheep was guarded by a young shepherd boy. One day he led the flock to graze in a green pasture, but a wolf came that day and attacked one of the sheep. The boy tried to frighten away the wolf, but the wolf sensed the young child was no threat. Soon the wolf devoured one sheep and turned his attention to another sheep. The young boy vainly tried to fight the wolf, but the wolf's bared teeth indicated to the youth that he would become part of the wolf's lunch. The boy knew he could not return to the village for help, for the wolf would scatter the sheep in his absence. If the wolf devoured or scattered the flock, the people of his village would starve the next winter, and he would be held responsible. He did the only thing he could think of, he fell to his knees and prayed to Allah that the wolf might be destroyed. He prayed that Allah would send angels with fire to kill the wolf.

It was 1943 in the desolate land of western Persia (modern day Iran). The American army placed the "Persian Gulf Command" on the railway lines leading up into Russia in order to protect American weapons and supplies being shipped up to the Eastern front. There Russian and German armies engaged in a herculean struggle in which millions died. For three years American soldiers watched endless train cars carry heavy armaments into Russia and stared at the desert wastes directly to the west of them. Sabotage of the railway by pro-German Arabs from Iraq had to be prevented, and though rare, it did happen. Americans quietly repaired and kept silent about any successful act of sabotage.

My father was a sergeant in command of a platoon at one of the rail stops. He was also the medic for the unit. Typical of the strange things that happened in World War II, as he was being processed through the lines to be sent overseas, someone noted that he worked in a Rexall Drug store before the war, and so he was handed a medical kit. "Gnuse, you're a medic now." He had no time to tell them that he was a "soda jerk" in the cafeteria part of the drug store. He made a good medic, though. So he was both the sergeant commanding the unit and the medic, and as such he accomplished some significant medical activities. But that is another story.

He routinely assigned two men to patrol the tracks every morning and afternoon at their little camp in the desert. So the soldiers walked up and down the tracks endlessly traversing this scrub wasteland of western Persia. To the east lay some rolling hills. After mindlessly walking up and down the track many times, two soldiers one day decided to walk for a couple of hours back into the hills. One of them was named "Hawk," because he was a marksman. He had hoped to be a sniper in combat, but instead he ended up patrolling the desert and staring down at the metal tracks of the rail lines. He longed to fire his rifle.

As they walked further up into the hills, they crossed over a ridge and beheld a beautiful little green valley in front of them.

On the other side of the valley was a small flock of sheep. "Let's go check it out," one of them said. "It's like a scene from the Bible." As they approached the flock they saw a wolf casually eating a sheep. Next to the wolf was a rather thoroughly consumed body of a sheep. On the other side of the flock was a little shepherd boy. He was on his knees, praying.

"Well, would you look at that!" said Hawk. "Watch this!," said Hawk, the marksman, who then bolted his M-1 rifle. One shot, the wolf was dead. Hawk was truly a marksman.

The little shepherd boy, perhaps eight years old, came running over to the American GIs yelling, "Fravashi, fravashi, fravashi!" He threw himself at their feet, face down, and continued to chant "Fravashi." He was happy and crying at the same time.

"Yeah, yeah, yeah. Sure kid. 'Frechevy' to you, too. Now go back to your sheep. Have a good day. Glad to be of help." Hawk then said to his buddy, "What do you think that word means."

"I dunno. Maybe it means thank you."

"Yeah," Hawk said, "that's probably what it means."

The Persian shepherd boy retreated crying and smiling, saying again and again, "Fravashi."

Back at the camp they told their story to the rest of the American soldiers. They asked what the word "Fravashi" could mean. Two little Persian boys who helped my father in his medical duties said, "A Fravashi is a very powerful angel."

"Really . . ." said Hawk, with a sarcastic grin. "That's the only time I'll ever be called an angel."

The little boys continued, "We believe that Fravashis serve Allah, that they are fair skinned angels who will come down at the judgment day and destroy evil with lightning bolts, and sometimes they will come down to help people in special need."

My father said, "It looks like you two guys were angels today."

"Ah, that's ridiculous," said Hawk.

My dad said, "No! Think about it. This little shepherd boy has never seen fair skinned Americans before, and he has never seen guns. He and his village have been in those hills for centuries with no outside contact. You walk over the hill, white Americans, with M-1 rifles, so, of course, you're angels with lightning sticks."

"Well, Gnuse, you may be right," said Hawk.

"Think about it some more," my dad said. "You came over that hill as a marksman with an M-1 rifle at the very moment the little boy was praying. You could kill the wolf with one shot, not just frighten him away, so that he would come back tomorrow. You're a marksman. What are the odds that in all the centuries that village has existed, that you would walk over that hill at precisely that moment?"

"Wow, Gnuse, that's almost enough to make me believe in God."

My dad said, "Who answered that little boy's prayer?"

"Whadda you mean?" said Hawk.

My dad continued, "Someone answered that little boy's prayer. Was it our God? Was it Allah? Or, is it the same God? Somebody answered that little boy's prayer."

"Gnuse, now you got me spooked."

John 10:16: "I have other sheep that do not belong to this fold. I must bring the also and they will listen to my voice."

Of whom does Jesus speak? If this were read and heard by Christians around 100 CE, when the gospel of John was written, with whom would the Christian audience associate those "other sheep?" Many early Christains felt that somehow God would also save non-Christians because of this and other passages in the Bible. Would this include Muslims, Hindus, Buddhists, and others?

Who answered the little Muslim boy's prayer? Or was it just a coincidence of monumental proportions? Does the God of the universe answer the prayers of little shepherd boys? Did God answer the prayer of that little Persian shepherd boy, as once the prayers of a little shepherd boy named David were answered? David killed

4

a wolf with a sling, then went on to kill Goliath back in 1000 BCE. In 1943 God decided to use an American GI with an M-1 rifle. Does God like little shepherd boys? Yahweh for David, Allah for the Persian shepherd boy, God for us—is it the same God? I think so. I think God likes little shepherds (among others, of course).

A postscript is worthy of note. Preachers like to steal good stories. My dad told me this story in the 1950s. I first told this as a sermon story in Doraville, Georgia in 1972, and repeatedly after that. I have since then heard it told by other preachers, most notably in 1992. Then it was a little Christian Arab boy as the shepherd and an Israeli soldier as the marksman—different context, slightly different meanings. I guess the Persian/Iranian setting didn't seem logical to later audiences. That's because history is stranger than fiction. Maybe you've heard the story yourself in different garb. Good stories evolve over the years.

A Doll Named Bippy

It was December, 1969, when the twenty-five guys in my dormitory decided to have a Christmas party for orphans. We were at Concordia Senior College in Fort Wayne, Indiana, a pre-ministerial college which was a feeder school for Concordia Seminary in St. Louis. Our dormitories were built like alpine lodges, holding a maximum of thirty-six students. Our number, twenty-five, was perfect for an orphan party, because we could invite twenty-five orphans, and each one of us could give a present to a particular orphan.

There was a Roman Catholic orphanage in the city, which we decided to call to obtain our twenty-five orphans. A number of us crowded around the guy who made the phone call to the orphanage. He spoke to the receptionist and said, "We would like to invite some orphans to our dormitory for a Christmas party." The woman at the other end asked, "How many would you like?" He said twenty-five. He then turned to us and said, "She showed no surprise, like this happens all the time. It's like ordering out for pizza!"

When she got the information on the time and the place, she assured us that they could provide us with twenty-five children. We then stipulated that we would like the more rowdy children, the ones that would be embarrassing if you sent them to someone's home. Obviously, the chief number of requests came from private homes over the holidays, and the orphanage sent children that would make a good impression. We said, "We're a bunch of guys in a dormitory, and we can handle children that you might not want to send to private homes." The woman said, "We can arrange that." When our orphans arrived for the party, they were mostly girls aged eight to eleven years old. We thought they made a mistake. But after the girls roasted marshmallows in our dormitory fireplace and proceeded to run around the dorm lounge with the sticky marshmallows on their sticks trying to put them in each other's long or curly hair, we understood. They also ran around the dormitory in and out of our dorm rooms. Nothing was lost, however. They were, after all, little ladies.

Each of us adopted an orphan by name in order to give that child a personal present. Everyone decided more or less what they wished to give his boy or girl, and then some of us went to Toys R Us to purchase twenty-five presents. While most of us were selecting our presents, we heard a basketball bouncing over in one part of the store. We walked over to find Tom bouncing a basketball, and he promptly said, "I think this is a perfect gift for my kid." Bill, his roommate, said, "Tom, you have an eight year-old girl, she won't want a basketball!" (Remember, this is 1969, we all gender stereotyped children, and adults too!) "Get her a doll or something like that."

Now Tom was 6'4" and an athlete. He played junior college basketball in Milwaukee, he was all-city football quarterback in high school in Milwaukee, and he also boxed Golden Gloves for a couple of years. His father was a Lutheran bishop in the upper midwest, and his three older brothers were all ministers. His dad sent him to pre-ministerial training, even though Tom did not want to be a clergyman. So that winter quarter, his junior year, he skipped all his classes so as to flunk out. He was a handsome, but rakish sort of fellow.

Tom found a doll. Bill said, "That's the ugliest doll in the universe!"

Tom said, "It is not. My kid will like it."

Bill said, "It's an ugly doll. Get another one."

Tom said, "It's a beautiful doll." This went on for some minutes.

Bill was correct in his assessment, but Tom bought the doll anyway. Thus, we left the store having purchased twenty-six presents. Yeah, Tom brought the basketball along, too. The dormitory fund paid for all the presents, including the basketball.

The day of the party came. A bus from the orphanage brought the kids, and two nuns came with them. We didn't count until later, but there were twenty-six kids. An additional child was added who had come into the orphanage that morning. He had been extracted from an abusive home situation rather quickly, and he was still dazed by the experience. He sat quietly with big sad eyes while a nun had her arm around him. We would discover him only when the presents were being handed out by Santa because he sat with that nun so quietly in the back of the dorm lounge throughout the party.

Gerald was Santa. He was 6'2" weighing well over two hundred pounds, and he had been an all-city center for Lutheran South High School in St. Louis. He didn't need pillows. When some of the boys hit him in the stomach, thinking that they were hitting pillows, they discovered that it was all him. Shocked, they said, "He has no pillows, he must be the real Santa." Gerald loved that.

The party was held in the dorm lounge where we had a fireplace for toasting marshmallows. Yeah, and that's when girls' hair got a little sticky. When the first little girl stuck her marshmallow in another girl's curly hair, she quickly gave her stick and marshmallow to another girl so as not to let the victim know who did it. Then she told the victim that there was marshmallow in her hair. Well, that started it. Girls began sticking marshmallows in each other's hair. You would think that male college students could stop this. No! No way! Brad, one of the more "gung-ho" students in our class, said of the offending girl, "Oh my gosh, she's gonna' grow up and be just like me!" For Brad that was a very appropriate statement.

They later scattered all over the dorm. I found one little girl in my room going back and forth to either side of the room lighting and extinguishing two candles with a third lit candle in her hand. She was doing it in a formal way. She was playing altar girl (which they didn't have in those days). She never saw me. I always wonder what happened to her. I wish I could have adopted her.

It came time to hand out the presents. Gerald did it in stately fashion, pulling them out of a large bag and reading off the child's name and telling who the giver was. He was a perfect Santa. Each child came forward to receive a present, thank the giver, and hurry back to his or her seat to excitedly open the toy. We then discovered that Tom's little girl was really a boy. A number of us were watching from the hallway into the lounge when we discovered this.

"Tom, Tom, your little girl is a boy. Go find that basketball and give it to him. Swap the presents in Santa's bag, and do it without being noticed." We told Gerald (aka "the real Santa") what we were doing, so he would slow down the dispensing of the presents. Tom sneaked in and exchanged the presents in Santa's bag. Okay, try to picture someone 6'4" sneaking around in a subtle and quiet fashion to swap presents in Santa's bag, as all the children watch Santa. We all breathed a sigh of relief when that was done.

Then we discovered that there was a twenty-sixth child. He sat with a nun, who had her arm around him. He had been withdrawn from an abusive home that morning and he was still rather shocked. The nuns thought a party like this would be good for him, but they did not know about the individualized presents. He would not get one; his large and sad eyes watched all the proceedings. As the presents were being handed out, the nun probably tried to comfort him gently and explain that he would not get one, for he had been brought to the party on such late notice. We could see tears in his eyes.

Out in the hall we panicked. "We need a present! What have we got to give him? We can't give him a bottle of Brad's gin!"

Tom said, "I can give him my philosophy textbook."

Bill said, "Nobody wants a textbook that's never been opened."

Some of us then said, "Tom, give him that doll that you just pulled out of Santa's bag for the basketball."

Someone said, "You can't give a doll to a boy." (Remember gender stereotyping in 1969.)

Another voice spoke, "It's all we have that's appropriate for a child."

Tom said, "Yeah, I'll give him the doll; it's already wrapped."

Bill quickly stated, "But it's an ugly doll!"

Tom said, "It's a beautiful doll." . . .

"Ugly doll." . . .

"Beautiful doll." . . .

"Ugly doll."

"Beautiful doll."

"Ugly doll."

"Shut up, both of you. Give him the damn doll. It's all we have."

Again 6'4" Tom quietly and gracefully tippy-toed in again to place the doll in Santa's bag.

Gerald had given all the presents away except that one. He dramatically said, "Well, I think that's all the presents. Oh, wait a minute. Here's one more." He called the little guy up and gave him the last present. He had been crying, especially as he viewed the almost empty sack, but suddenly now he became very happy.

He went back to his seat next to the nun and opened the present. Immediately he began to cry and sob, hug the doll, and say, "Bippy, bippy, bippy." The nun next to him was wide-eyed with her mouth hanging open as she looked at the doll.

Tom was out in the hall with the rest of us. "Tom go back in there and find out what this Bippy business is about." So he did.

As soon as Tom walked up to the nun she began to say excitedly, "How did you know? You couldn't have known. It's not possible. How did you do it? How did you know?"

"Know what?" said Tom.

She responded, "This is his lovey! This is his favorite toy! We took him this morning so quickly that his lovey was left behind. This is Bippy! This is his lovey! He was distraught that we did not bring his lovey. You found his lovey! You gave him back his lovey! How did you do it? It's not possible that you could have known! How did you do it?"

Tom was silent for a moment, standing there looking rather stunned. For he, after all, had chosen the doll in the toy store. He, more than she, may have been stunned. Then he said, "Well, Sister, ...maybe there really is a God."

When he came back out into the hall with us, we asked him what he found out. He said, "I discovered that there really is a God."

The party was a success. A good time was had by all. We cleaned the marshmallows off the floor and the furniture. The juniors decided they would do this again next year.

Footnote: I do not know what ultimately happened to that little boy and Bippy. But Tom ultimately did go to seminary, graduate, and served as a pastor in Lutheran churches for many years.

Mark 5:22–23, 35–36, 40–42: (22) Then one of the leaders of the synagogue named Jairus came and, when he saw him, fell at his feet (23) and begged him repeatedly, "My little daughter is at the point of death. Come and lay your hands one her, so that she may be made well, and live." (35) While he was still speaking, some people came from the leader's house to say, "Your daughter is dead. Why trouble the teacher any further?" (36) But overhearing what they said, Jesus said to the leader of the synagogue, "Do not fear, only believe." (40) Then he put them all outside, and took the child's father and mother and those who were with him, and went in where the child was. (41) He took her by the hand and said to her, "Talitha cum," which means, "Little girl, get up!" (42) And immediately the girl got up and began to walk about (she was twelve years of age). At this they were overcome with amazement.

In the days of Jesus, infant mortality was about 50 percent, and of those who survived, perhaps only half made it to their teen-age years. The ancient Israelites and Jews loved their children, but they knew that too often their children would die. So, they accepted it. The rest of society thus did not pay that much attention to children, a vulnerable segment of the population, and a segment of society that one could not regard as having too much value. Times were harsh then. Jesus raised a small child from the dead and thus made a statement to his contemporaries about the value of a small person's life.

Perhaps our modern age might not pay much attention to orphans or those removed from abusive homes. Jesus did and still does. We should also. Many children worldwide starve and suffer from disease, and too many of those live homeless in war. Too few people in our society seem to care. Jesus cares. We should also.

Perhaps at Christmas time God has a certain sense of humor, or perhaps it might be a rogue little angel at times. At any rate, a small sign was given with a doll named Bippy. A small child, lost in the world like a bit of flotsam on the ocean surface, had a priceless gift given to him. This sign meant something to us who were there. May the children in our world receive a symbolic gift like Bippy.

The Lenten Goose

Little is known about Saint Felicitatis, who is not to be confused with Felicitas of Rome who lived fifty years earlier. Felicitatis was the servant or slave to Perpetua and both women were martyred in Carthage of North Africa in 203 CE under emperor Septimus Serverus. We know too little about them, so scholars debate the details and the dates. Both women were recent converts to Christianity in this apparently regional persecution in North Africa. They refused to recant their beliefs, as so many Christians in North Africa did. In fact, Perpetua was baptized in prison. Perpetua's father, a pagan, pleaded with her to recant her Christian faith, but she refused. We hear nothing about Felicitatis or Felicity in this process. Both died heroically, steadfastly refusing to recant. They are heroes and appropriately regarded as saints in the Christian tradition.

It was the spring semester of my first year in seminary, 1971. I lived on the second floor of a dormitory on campus with a roommate whom I knew since high school. In the two rooms next to ours were four other students who had been together in the pre-ministerial training system since high school. Most of the other guys on that floor at least knew each other from our junior and senior years in college. So we were all pretty close friends.

At the end of the hall there was a seminarian who was new to the educational system; none of us knew him before. He was short and dumpy, a very friendly and smiling guy, who cheerfully said hello to everyone he passed. He was Martin. Martin always wore black clerical clothes and a collar, which most of us did not, and he seemed a little eccentric. Not eccentric in a bad way, but in a nice way. He also wore a little black beret all the time. Someone nicknamed him Friar Tuck.

One day Martin came down the hall from his room at the far end of the hall away from the stairwell, and he had a goose on a leash. The goose walked very obediently in front of Martin almost as if he or she were trained.

"Martin, why the goose?" one of us asked.

"This is Saint Felicitatis, and she is my Lenten goose." Well, indeed, Ash Wednesday had just passed that week, so it was Lent. "When Lent is over, I intend to cook and eat her for Easter."

There was a silent and uncomfortable pause. "Really," I said.

"Yes, indeed. She will observe the vigil of Lent, and then I will cook and eat her. She is an Easter goose." There was more silence among us. Then Martin said, "Come along Saint Felicitatis, we must go to class now." He moved down the hall as we stood there in silence.

After he went down the stairwell, we said among ourselves, "Well, we always knew he was eccentric."

One of said, "He's such a cheery fellow. That's a little ghoulish."

I observed, "Saint Felicitatis was a famous martyr in Carthage around 200 CE. When I heard the name, I thought immediately that this isn't going to end well."

Martin went down the sidewalk to the classroom building, a long walk, since our dorm was the farthest residence away from the main campus. People along the way would stop and ask him, "Why do you have a goose on a leash?"

His response was the same. "This is Saint Felicitatis, my Lenten goose. I intend to cook and eat her for Easter Sunday dinner." The usual response was silence.

Saint Felicitatis went to class and stayed by Martin's side on the leash. Of course, professors would ask the question, "What is that goose doing in the classroom?"

Martin would respond, "This is Saint Felicitatis, and she is my Lenten goose. At the end of the Lenten vigil, I will cook her and eat her for Easter dinner." I don't believe that any professor had a follow up question to that. Professors generally did not push questions with students who appeared to be somewhat eccentric.

Throughout the rest of the Lenten season Martin and Felicitatis became a regular sight on campus. No one asked the questions anymore. We just observed him with quiet bemusement. He was quite the sight—in his black clerical clothing with a white goose on a leash in front of him.

Well, Easter came and passed. We were in the dorm when Martin came strolling down the hall that week, sans Saint Felicitatis.

"Martin, where's the goose? Where is Saint Felicitatis? Did you cook her and eat her?" one of us asked.

"I took Saint Felicitatis to the big lake in Forest Park, from where you can see the art museum. I showed her the lake, I pointed out the ducks in the lake along with a couple of swans, and I pointed out to her what a beautiful blue sky was overhead on that Easter Sunday. Then I took off her leash and told her to fly away. 'You are free, Saint Felicitatis! You are free! You are no longer under the sentence of death! It is Easter! Jesus is risen, and you are free!' Felicitatis then waddled down to the water and swam away. She didn't fly, but waddling off was good enough. That was her resurrection." Martin then walked down the dormitory hallway in his usual cheery, bouncy manner.

We stood there silently. "Well, he sure fooled us," one of us said.

"The goose, too," said someone else.

"He's a genius."

"Well, he's something."

"I think there's a sermon in there somewhere."

Ephesians 2:1–2, 4–5: (1) You were dead through the trespasses and sin (2) in which you once lived following the course of this world, ... (4) But God, who is rich in mercy, out of the great love with which he loved us, (5) even when we were dead through our trespasses, made us alive together with Christ.

Martin's Lenten goose lived under the sentence of death, just as do we, when we are dead through trespasses and sin. We contemplate our finitude and our sinful weakness during the season of Lent. But as the goose was freed on Easter, so we also are freed by the resurrection of Jesus which conquers sin, death, and evil. We celebrate Easter so often, once a year, in fact, that we begin to take all the language and imagery for granted. Eccentric Martin brought it back to life for us dramatically. What about St. Felicitatis? I supposed she was swimming somewhere contentedly on the lake in Forest Park snatching bread crumbs that tourists threw into the lake for the aquatic fowl.

Siberian Lutherans

The parable of the mustard seed always evokes references to periods of rapid growth of the Christian church, especially on the mission field. But my favorite example is a story told to us students in seminary by a visiting professor, Bishop Stephen Neil, Anglican bishop from South India, who reported to us a story told to him by Hans Lilje a few years earlier. Lilje was at that time retired (1970s), but he had been the president of the Lutheran World Federation, an organization that many Lutheran denominations belong to in a somewhat unofficial status. So he was the closest thing that Lutherans have to a Lutheran pope. The thing that impressed us the most was not that he had been president of the LWF, but that he had spent three years in a German concentration camp for his refusal to cooperate with Hitler in manipulating the Lutheran Church in Germany. That earned our respect above all. The headquarters of the LWF have been in Geneva, Switzerland for many years.

Hans Lilje told Stephen Neil of how he visited Siberia in the 1970s when the Soviet Union allowed the LWF to make contact with Lutherans in Siberia who had formed a rather loosely knit organization called the Siberian Lutheran Church. The church was formed out of exiles who had been sent to Siberia in the 1930s by Stalin. They were essentially ethnic Germans from the Ukraine who were purged by Stalin, along with most everybody else in the Ukraine. Their clergy had been killed or imprisoned, so they found themselves in Siberia without clergy and forced to reorganize themselves with lay leadership. There were about one hundred thousand who were sent into exile in the 1930s and they were scattered about in this area of Siberia, where they apparently regrouped and met in people's homes under lay leadership. They were still there thirty years later surviving as a semi-organized group of church folk.

So Lilje and a few other church officials from Geneva flew into Tashkent in Siberia and were met by the leader of the Siberian Lutheran Church. He was an old, gaunt, tall steelworker from Tashkent, who was very quiet and very somber. The group went to a small meeting hall, where the first thing they asked of Lilje was to preach a sermon. Since they had not had a trained clergyman for many years, this was a symbolic gesture.

As they sat down at the table to speak, Lilje wondered how many of the one hundred thousand Lutherans from the Ukraine were left after thirty years. He had hoped to send trained clergy from Germany to minister to their scattered communities. The Soviet government had given them permission to do that. Lilje thought to himself not only about how many were left, but how far afield they might be scattered in that area of Siberia. He wondered if it would take about three, or five, or maybe even seven clergy to travel about and serve these parishes.

Meanwhile, the grizzled old steelworker slowly spoke about their home churches. He said that more than just Lutherans attended these meetings. "We have Greek Orthodox, Baptists, Pentecostals, Methodists, Roman Catholics, and even non-believers come to our meetings." Lilje wondered, were there two thousand, five thousand, how many? Finally, the old man said, "In our humble little house churches, we have about one million people who attend on a regular or occasional basis." Lilje was stunned. He said the only thing he could think of was the saying of Jesus, when he was told to silence his disciples, responded by saying that if his disciples were silenced, then the very stones would speak out. At the same time, his chief assistant from the LWF leaned over and said to him, "Herr pastor, we can go home now, they don't need us, they don't need us at all." From one hundred thousand people this little church without clergy grew to one million folk. What an incredible testimony this was to the faith and determination of those exiles.

After telling us this story that he had received from Lilje, Neil looked at us seminarians in St. Louis in the early 1970s and said, "Gentlemen, you are privileged to be ministers, but never think that the church needs you. If you were to disappear overnight, God would raise up stones to replace you. And some of those 'stones' would preach better sermons than you." And to what Neil said, I would add that those stones would also have apostolic succession, because it comes from God also.

Matthew 13:31–32: "The Kingdom of heaven is like a mustard seed that someone took and sowed in his field; it is the smallest of all the seeds, but when it has grown it is the greatest of shrubs and becomes a tree, so that the birds of the air come and make nests in its branches."

The mustard seed is an image that has often described what God has done in our world with the Christian movement. It is also a story that can be recounted to individuals, people, and churches especially that underestimate their capacity to accomplish great things for the kingdom.

Sometimes, if we think our actions don't matter, recall those many times in church history when a small group of people accomplished so very much. Never underestimate yourself, never underestimate what you might do with a few other people working together.

Elizabeth of Hungary

Once upon a time there was a little princess and she was married to a handsome prince. She left her parents' home to live with her husband in Germany. They lived in a beautiful castle high upon a hill in the city where her husband ruled. She and her ladies would walk down the hill to the village below to visit the marketplace regularly. That is where our story begins.

It is the year 1221. Yes, the story begins like a fairy tale, but it is a real story. This young princess and her ladies would go down into the village to visit the market regularly, but as they did so, they also saw the poor and the sick people in the village down in the valley. In 1223 she came in contact with the teachings of St. Francis and they inspired her to help the poor. She would take the poor in the valley, in the city, food and clothing, and she even built a hospital for the sick, the ruins of which can still be seen today.

Her husband was a devout Christian who supported his wife's generosity, even though she used up most of her dowry and much of his wealth by helping the poor. He knew she was doing the will of God and he loved her very much. However, some of the relatives, including her husband's brother, were concerned that she would give away all of their family's wealth to the poor.

In 1227 her husband died of a fever in Italy on his way to the Sixth Crusade. The princess was heart-broken. Now that she was a widow, her brother-in-law took over the administration of the castle and the family wealth. Her generosity came to an end. She argued in vain with her brother-in-law. She left the castle and went to a convent, but even then she would sneak out to go back and help at the hospital she had built. In 1231 she died, perhaps of a fever she caught ministering at the hospital.

The rest of the family was sad, but they said that it was a shame that she wasted so much money on the poor. She and her husband could have taken their place among the powerful nobility of Germany, but alas that would not happen. They probably sat around and said that she and her husband could have become famous, but instead they would be forgotten forever. If we listen closely, perhaps we can hear them say, "Her name will be forgotten forever."

Her name was Elizabeth. She has not been forgotten.

In Marburg, Germany today there is a hugh cathedral that is the center of life in the town. The University of Marburg holds concerts and other artistic events there, and every Advent there is an Advent Market surrounding the cathedral. Built in the fourteenth century, it is still a place of worship for the Lutherans of Marburg. It is called St. Elizabeth's Church after that little girl who helped the poor. They have not forgotten her. Next to the church are the ruins of the hospital that she built, and the ruins are tended by the citizens of Marburg. They have not forgotten her.

On November 17 and 19 she is variously celebrated as a saint by Roman Catholics, Anglicans, and Lutherans. She has not been forgotten. It is a date before Thanksgiving, a day that many Christians celebrate by giving food baskets to the poor.

The relatives of Elizabeth who said that she would be forgotten have been forgotten. Germany no longer has nobility, but it has the Cathedral named after the little girl who gave so much, including herself, to the poor.

If you go to Marburg today, perhaps at night on the hill just below the old palace, you might see the wisps of young women walking down the hill. They are dressed in medieval garb. Look closely, for it is Elizabeth and her ladies. They are taking food to the poor. Look in the distance, further down the hill. There is a man. He is Jewish. He is calling upon the young ladies to follow him down into the valley. It is Jesus.

Matthew 25:34–36: (34) "Then the king will say to those at his right hand, 'Come, you that are blessed by my Father, inherit the kingdom prepared for you from the foundation of the world; (35) for I was hungry and you gave me food, I was thirsty and you gave me something to drink, I was a stranger and you welcomed me, (36) I was naked and you gave me clothing, I was sick and you took care of me, I was in prison and you visited me.' . . . (40) And the king will answer them, 'Truly I tell you, just as you did it to one of the least of these who are members of my family, you did it to me.'"

Princess Elizabeth understood the message of Jesus; the nobility in her family did not. For them power, prestige, and wealth were what mattered in life. She is remembered for her Christian convictions; they are forgotten. Do we, like her, understand what our Lord calls us to do in this world? This parable of Jesus too often seems to be forgotten by Christians in our affluent western society, especially as so many human beings suffer privation in the rest of our world.

Hans Walter Wolff's Story

Hans Walter Wolff was a famous Old Testament scholar in Germany. In 1973 he came to my Lutheran seminary in St. Louis to teach a couple of courses for the fall semester. I was fortunate to take both courses, one in the prophet Hosea and the other in Old Testament anthropology. In both he used textbooks that he had written. He came into class the first day and all of us American students stood up and said, "Guten morgen, Der Herr Professor." We thought we would be respectful like students in Germany. He became very embarrassed and said, "Don't do that. My students in Germany do that, and I tell them not to do it either."

Wolff was a kind and gentle man, who would treat all students with respect and entertain all questions. He would hold the door open for the nuns who came over from St. Louis University to take classes in our Protestant seminary. They often arrived late and he would jump up to hold the door for them and greet them. He would advance his own opinion, voiced in the textbooks he wrote and which we used in class, by saying, "This is what I think. Perhaps, I am wrong. You can decide for yourself." He was a very humble man for being such a world renowned scholar.

One day he brought in a three volume history of Baroque music, which he found in our library. He was so happy that he almost cried, for the books were written by his son. He was so proud.

Another student in the class, Bill, once turned to me and said, "So this is the great Hans Walter Wolff, the famous German Professor. He's just a cute little old man!"

He and his wife stayed in an apartment near the seminary, and they would routinely invite about eight students at a time to come to their apartment for beer, cheese, and crackers. He would talk about various aspects of his scholarship and other matters.

When my group was at his apartment, he spoke about research he did on Exodus 1 some thirty-five years prior. He spoke of how he read the story about the midwives who defied pharaoh and would not kill the baby Israelite boys at their birth. Instead, they defied pharaoh by saying Israelite women were stronger than Egyptian women, and immediately after childbirth the Israelite women would go out and work before the midwives arrived. Wolff concluded that even though the midwives had Hebrew sounding names, they must have been Egyptian by virtue of their ability to compare Israelite and Egyptian women critically the way they did before pharaoh (and he believed them). Wolff was famous for this particular theory.

He then began to talk about how that story gave him a great revelation. The Egyptian women protected the babies of the foreigners and defied their own ruler, who was for them a god incarnate. Pharaoh was the living god Horus for Egyptians. These women, who were poor and probably slaves, defied their mighty ruler because they knew it was wrong to kill babies. Their courage was great. Wolff said, "I wish my people had done that in the past generation. You Americans do not realize how great their act of rebellion was to defy pharaoh in that way. For your nation was born in an act of rebellion two hundred years ago, rebellion is natural for you. We see your elections as a form of rebellion. We Germans, however, were raised with a sense of absolute obedience to our God-given rulers, even if they are less than perfect. *Ehr* ("honor") and *Furcht* ("fear") is what we were taught to affirm when it came to obedience to those in authority. But these women opposed their divine ruler because they feared God more and they would not kill the foreign babies. Israel was born in an act of rebellion by two slave women. This changed my way of thinking. I became active in politics and sought to protect the rights of those who were not German. I even became involved in some very dangerous political activity." Wolff paused for a moment. Then he said, "I always wish that they had caught me instead of my friend Dietrich."

We seminarians froze. We knew who Dietrich was. He was Dietrich Bonhoeffer, a German Lutheran theologian, who was executed in a concentration camp by the Nazis in 1945 because he somehow participated in the bomb plot against Adolph Hitler even while he was in prison. A plot created by six German generals and about ten Lutheran clergy attempted to kill Adolph Hitler with a bomb carried into a meeting of the German High Command. Colonel Claus Von Stauffenberg brought the bomb into the meeting in a briefcase. It exploded, but unfortunately it threw the meeting table on top of Hitler, and though it killed other military personnel, Hitler survived. All the military people and half of the Lutheran clergy involved in the plot were captured and executed, including Dietrich Bonhoeffer, in 1944 and 1945. Bonhoeffer wrote his famous *Letters from Prison* during his imprisonment.

But some of the clergy were never apprehended, and people in Germany did not know who they were after the war. They stayed silent in Germany even after the war fearing it was not safe to admit what they did.

Wolff had just admitted that he was involved in the bomb plot and was never caught. My friend, who almost dropped his beer, turned to me and said, "Did I call Wolff a cute little old man. He tried to kill Hitler!" Yes, he did. He did it because he was inspired by a story in Exodus 1.

Well, that's what the Bible will do to you, if you read it closely, it is dangerous. It took a "cute little old man," or at that time I suppose he was a "cute young man," and it sent him after one of the greatest tyrants of all time. It will give you the courage of those Egyptian midwives. Read the Bible closely, and you take big risk, for it may change your life.

Exodus 1:15–21: (15) The king of Egypt said to the Hebrew midwives, one of whom was named Shiphrah and the other Puah, (16) "When you act as midwives to the Hebrew women, and see them on the birthstool, if it is a boy, kill him; but if it is a girl, she shall live." (17) But the midwives feared God; they did not do as the king of Egypt commanded them, but they let the boys live. (18) So the king of Egypt summoned the midwives and said to them, "Why have you done this, and allowed the boys to live?" (19) The midwives said to Pharaoh, "Because the Hebrew women are not like the Egyptian women; for they are vigorous and give birth before the midwife comes to them." (20) So God dealt well with the midwives; and the people multiplied and became very strong. (21) And because the midwives feared God, he gave them families.

Would we have the courage to stand up like the midwives did? They stood up to their leader, whom they considered an incarnation of the Egyptian god Horus. Of course, we do not face a tyrant like pharaoh of Egypt or Adolph Hitler of Germany. But it still takes determination to help the poor in our own age, especially starving children found throughout the world, or abused children found everywhere, including our own country, unfortunately. Are we willing to support a campaign that provides more money for public education in our community? There are many ways for us to help children who suffer or are disadvantaged in our modern world. Do we have the courage to stand up for them?

Silly Goose

We use expressions like, "You silly goose!," or "He or she doesn't have the sense God gave a goose!" But are those statements really appropriate? Do we malign geese unfairly?

Geese fly in a V-formation because each goose creates a drafting effect on the goose behind him or her. By flying in this V-formation the entire group of geese add an additional 70 percent of flying distance to their flying efforts than if each goose flew individually. (We similarly can draft in our car if we follow closely behind a semi-trailer, which is not really too safe.). When a goose falls out of the V-formation, he or she will feel the drag of the air, and quickly get back into the formation. When the lead goose tires, that goose goes back into the formation and another goose takes the lead. Geese honk to encourage the leader to maintain the speed of the entire formation. The entire flying formation is a powerful symbol of group cooperation.

This is what is most interesting. When a goose becomes ill or is wounded (by a hunter most likely) and drops out of the formation, two other geese will fly down to the earth to help or protect the weakened goose. Those two geese will stay with the affected goose until that goose can fly or until the goose dies. They then return to the skies and join another formation as it comes along.

I suppose that if some individual goose failed in these responsibilities, the other geese might say, "He doesn't have the heart that God gave a human."

We would do well to imitate geese in these ways. They work as a team, take turns with the leadership roles, support their leaders, and they assist each other when ill or injured. Silly geese, they have the virtues we too often lack.

1 Thessalonians 5:11: Therefore, encourage one another and build one another up.

We live in an age of competition, cutthroat competition. People compete with others in the business world, in the office, in politics, in sports, in academic competition, contests, and in so many human activities. Children even compete for their parents' affection. We have become obsessed with competition and winning, almost at every level in our lives. We see competition even in church life. Too often we do not work like a team, and sometimes an individual will sabotage a group effort for personal advantage. The New Testament so many times encourages Christians to work together for the good of the group, and we need to heed this message.

The Man Who Planted Trees

Jean Giono tells the story about a shepherd who lived alone in a desolate part of the French countryside with only his sheep for companions. Every day the shepherd would go forth with his flock to some hilly area near his stone cottage and take with him one hundred acorns carefully chosen from among a larger number of acorns. Giono stayed with him one night in 1913 after walking through much of this desolate land, and he observed the shepherd selecting one hundred acorns from a large bag of acorns that he had. Curious as to what the shepherd was doing, Giono walked with him the next day i to observe him carefully poking a hole in the ground with an iron rod and then carefully placing an acorn in it. The shepherd told Giono that he had been doing this for over three years and estimated that he had planted over one hundred thousand trees. The shepherd said that he expected about one-fourth of the trees to grow to a significant size, and they would provide forestation for this desolate area in the French country-side. Over the next thirty some years Giono visited the shepherd three times. By the third visit Giono observed that in some areas where the shepherd had planted acorns, and later the seeds of Beech trees, villages had come into existence, in the presence of a verdant forest, which had arisen from those initial seedlings. The shepherd's name was Elzéard Bouffier. He died in a hospice in 1947. During his life through patience, persistence, and dedication he planted hundreds of thousands of trees, created forests where none had been before, and permitted the emergence of thriving new French villages. Jean Giono tells his story in "The Man who Planted Trees" (*Country Living*, March, 1997, pp. 120-21, 164-65, 188).

Matthew 13:31–32: (31) He put before them another parable: "The Kingdom of heaven is like a mustard seed that someone took and sowed in his field; (32) it is the smallest of all the seeds, but when it has grown it is the greatest of shrubs and becomes a tree, so that the birds of the air come and make nests in its branches."

This story speaks to us, clergy and laity, about patience in our work in the church, and how diligence, hard work, and dogged persistence can sometimes yield a great harvest. The shepherd did not expect immediate results; he knew that it would take years for the results to shine forth as verdant forests. Trees are like that. The parable of the mustard seed speaks of something small that becomes something quite large; just as the little acorns would become mighty oak trees. From small efforts great results may come in time. From our humble but persistent actions of Christian love, great things can eventually grow, if we are patient in our labors of love.

Folklore Stories

I CALL THESE ACCOUNTS Folklore because they might have happened somewhere at some time. They are realistic accounts. But as they stand, the stories are generic; they have begun to evolve in symbolic accounts in a timeless setting. Names are lost, place names are lost. These are memories that are evolving into folklore, symbolic narratives. Their symbolic nature makes them perfect as sermon stories or illustrations.

The Small Puppy

A small boy in a pet store walked over to where some new puppies were kept in a large box. A sign above the box advertised the puppies for sale. He gently picked each one up and held it, looking closely at each one. He asked the owner what one particular puppy cost. The owner quoted a price that was the same price for each of the little puppies. "I'll be back soon with the money," the small boy said with enthusiasm.

"Hurry," said the owner, "puppies sell quickly."

The boy said, "I'm not worried, the one I like will still be here."

He asked his parents for jobs to do in their house and the neighbors for odd jobs to do in their yards so that he could earn the money. He threw himself into the housework and the yardwork with real zeal. After only a few days of hard work he had the money, and he rushed back to the pet shop. He arrived at the pet shop and reaching into the box, which had only a few puppies left, he lifted out the one he had seen earlier, for it was still there.

"Oh," said the shop owner, "you probably don't want that one. He has a bad leg. Pick out a different puppy. This puppy can never run and play with you. He's crippled."

"That's okay, mister, I like him the best of all. I liked him when I first saw him."

The shop owner said, "Are you positive about that?"

"He's special to me," replied this little boy.

The shop owner said, "Okay. Then he's the puppy for you."

The boy purchased the little puppy. The little puppy wiggled with delight in the boy's hands, for few people had held the puppy before. As the boy left the store tenderly cradling his new little friend, the shop owner's eye caught sight of a leg brace underneath the boy's pant leg. He understood now. The little boy knew how it felt to be special.

2 Corinthians 12:9: But he said to me, "My grace is sufficient for you, for power is made perfect in weakness."

Many people have disabilities. The secret in life is not only do you cope well with the burden in life that has been given to you, but do you use it to your advantage in some way. Many people have done that in their lives, and as a result their weakness becomes a strength. My early childhood was one of much illness which confined me to bed. Lying in bed I did a tremendous amount of reading in history and science. My later academic success would not have been possible without this extensive reading. In our story the leg disability of the little boy has made him a special sort of person. He identified with that little dog, and he certainly did not let his leg prevent him from doing all the chores necessary for earning the money to buy that little dog. Can each of us use our limitations, our weaknesses, or even our failures to a greater advantage?

The Winter Field

Sven had come from Norway as a young man in the early twentieth century. On the boat he met a young girl who had been orphaned during the ship journey. She had been travelling with her grandfather, but he had died on the trip from an unexpected heart attack. Like Sven, Magda was Norwegian. Sven took her under his care. They developed a close relationship on board. Upon landing in New York, Magda had nowhere to go, so Sven asked her to come with him. He had made arrangements to purchase land for farming out in Iowa. She followed him out to Iowa.

Those first few years were difficult. Sven built a barn first, since they would need that for the farm animals, and they slept in the hay loft and made love there. After a time they were married in the local Lutheran church. Eventually they built a small house, but they would never forget those nights of passionate love in that hay loft. After living and working hard together, they began to reap the fruit of their hard labor. Sven worked hard and was a successful farmer on the Iowa plains.

They had seven children, three of them died at birth or very young, and they were buried in a small little cemetery plot in their back-yard. Magda kept flowers in that little cemetery continually. Their life was good, they were successful farmers, and they had four children who married and had children of their own. That family farm was the center of many family reunions and the heart of the greater family.

But time moves forward, Sven and Magda grew old, and then, Magda passed away. Sven was heartbroken. He planned to bury Magda in the little cemetery behind their home, for she had always said that she wished to be buried on the land where her children were laid.

The wake was held in Sven's home, in the living room. All their neighbors were there, for Sven and Magda were well loved in the community, very active in the local Lutheran church, and very generous in their dealings with others in the community.

During the wake, the county coroner and sheriff came to the home. The gave their heart-felt sympathy to Sven, and then they asked when they might come by and pick up Magda's body to take to the local cemetery.

Sven said, "Oh, no, I will bury Magda with her children behind our home, as she desired."

They said, "You cannot do that Sven, city health ordinances forbid that. Your children were buried there years ago before we had these health guidelines. You cannot bury a body on your own property anymore. We are sorry, but that's the law. We will come for your wife's body tomorrow morning."

Sven began to cry. "We have lived on this land since we were teenagers together, we loved and labored here, this land is our soul, heart, and body. We came here poor and worked hard together on this farm. We raised our children here; we buried our children here. She will be buried here. I will bury her myself. I will bury her here, as she wished."

They said, "Sven, if you bury her, we will find her. It is winter, and the the ground is hard. There will be evidence of a newly buried body in loose soil and a burial will be very easy to see."

Sven cried, "I will plow my field and you will not find her."

They responded, "Sven, you are old, and you cannot plow up that much land and bury Magda's body in one night. We will find her body, we will dig her up, and we will take her."

They left with Sven standing silently by Magda's body with tears in his eyes. The neighbors all stood around in the living room equally quiet after what they had heard. Slowly they left his home one by one in somber quietness.

The next morning the coroner and his assistants came to Sven's home. Though it was cold, he sat in his rocking chair on the front porch. "We have come for Magda's body," they said.

"I buried her in our yard," Sven quietly stated.

"We told you not to do that. We will find her," they sternly said.

They walked through Sven's house and walked out into his back yard. But as they looked around they saw that all of Sven's farmland had been plowed. Eight acres of land had been plowed up during that winter night.

"This is not possible," they said. "One old man with one tractor cannot plow up this much land in one winter night."

Sven quietly responded, "One tractor cannot, but twenty tractors can."

Silently they came, driving their tractors down the road, and methodically they began plowing his land, until Sven could respectfully bury Magda. I suppose they all broke the law. But sometimes there are higher values, and sometimes civil disobedience can serve a moral cause.

James 4:17. Anyone, then, who knows the right thing to do and fails to do it, commits sin.

Genesis 38:26. Then Judah acknowledged them and said, "She is more in the right than I."

The little farmers all knew what was the right thing to do. Maybe they broke the law, but they knew what was right. They helped their friend in need. The ancient sage Hillel once said that in order to keep a command of Torah, sometimes you do something that might appear to break it (30 BCE). In the Genesis 38 story Tamar has broken the law, but she did so because she was deprived of her rights as a widow, and Judah acknowledges her to be more "righteous" (the actual Hebrew) than he is. Sometimes breaking a law may entail keeping a higher law. Americans recognize this in their historic acceptance of free speech, demonstrations, and protest.

Little Birds in a Country Barn

The bright winter sun shone across the blanket of snow covering the fields of Fred's farm. A few months prior, rows of corn were harvested, leaving barren fields, until a heavy snowfall covered those fields with a white robe that glistened whenever the sun shone brightly in those South Dakota skies. The effect of the glistening snow was beautiful, so much better than the appearance of snow in the small nearby town where cars would drive over the snow until it was a blackened and a dirty looking mush of ice, water, and crunched snow. The shine on the snow could blind you if the sun were bright in the sky, especially about mid-day, when the rays of the sun shone more directly on the white earth beneath. The entire image added a depth of meaning to the concept of bright, shining light, especially when you faced the problem of snow glare or even snow blindness, while working out in the fields without sunglasses.

It was not that bright at 4:00 pm, which in the late winter time was actually close to sunset. The sun glare off the snow was beautiful, providing strong light in the land all around Fred's farm. It was Christmas eve, and the shining light off the snow was appropriate. Fred's wife certainly thought so. She felt that it was like the light of God coming into the world, something her fellow church members would celebrate that Christmas eve. Jesus was the light of the world, symbolized by the sun, and this white light reflected off of the snow was so aptly present for them as they drove to their Christmas Eve service.

"Fred," she said, "why don't you come to church this evening. The Christmas Eve service is beautiful with all those pretty red flowers. They complement the Christmas tree with its fine ornaments and all those beautiful lights around the church. You never come to church during the year, why don't you at least come for Christmas eve. Everyone in the area will be there. Pastor Bieber will preach a grand sermon."

"Eleanor," he said, "you know I don't believe in all that stuff. Yeah, maybe there's a God out there. But the idea that God came into the world as a little baby is nothing more than an entertaining tale told by first century country bumpkins in Palestine. Go and have a good time, I will stay here and do something meaningful. I will read my newspaper." Eleanor sadly left for church, as she did so many times in the past.

As Fred sat in his soft chair reading the *Chicago Tribune*, he heard noises outside. It was winter, with snow on the ground, so not much should be out there in the yard. The animals were all safely in their hog confinement pens and cow stables. He walked out onto the porch and realized that the sound came from the barn. So he went out to the barn, and as he approached the barn, the noise increased.

The noise was the sound of chirping birds. But more than chirping, they were birds in distress making frantic cries. As he entered the barn, he saw dozens of birds frantically flying back and forth in the barn rafters, the big open space of the barn, and into the small corners and crannies of the barn. They were making quite the racket. "Confounded birds," he said, "I don't know how they got into the barn, but apparently they don't have the good sense to get out of the barn." So he opened the barn doors wide apart for them to fly out. But none of the birds would fly toward the door. The bright outside light, especially augmented by the glare off of the snow, intimidated them. They flew even more into the dark recesses of the barn. "Don't fly away from the light, you silly birds. Don't fly into the darkness! Fly to the doors, fly to the light, fly away from the darkness. If you fly to the light, you will escape and be outside. You will be free." But, of course, the birds did not understand what he said, and he could not speak Bird.

Fred got up into the second level of the barn and tried to shoo them out. But this only made the birds more frantic, because he was big, loud, and moving among them while swinging a broom at them. Some began to fly into the barn walls and were obviously hurting themselves. "You silly birds, I'm trying to help you. I'm trying to help you escape the barn and the darkness. Fly to the light, fly to the light." The birds would not.

Fred went back down to the first floor and tried to show them how to escape by hopping out the barn door into the light and waving his arm for them to follow him. The birds were unimpressed, and they did not understand human pantomime. Fred stood in the barn and shook his head. "Of course, they don't understand me. I'm a human and they're birds. They cannot understand what humans say or do, we are too big and terrifying for them. If only I could become a bird, and fly among them for a time. They would get to trust me, and then many of them might follow me when I fly toward the light and out the door. If I could become one of them, I could show them the way out of the darkness into the light. I could save them."

Just as Fred had finished saying those words, the church bells rang, announcing the beginning of the Christmas Eve service. He suddenly realized what he had said, and his mind was stunned by the insight of his own words. He fell to his knees and began to cry.

John 1:1, 5, 14, 16. In the beginning was the Word, and the Word was with God, and the Word was God. . . . The Light shines in the darkness, and the darkness did not overcome it. . . . And the Word became flesh and lived among us. . . . From his fullness, we have received grace upon grace.

Fred wished to enter into the world of the birds and become a bird in order to lead them to the light. This is the language of the entire Gospel of John. Chapter 1 of John is a hymn, inspired by both Genesis 1 and Proverbs 8. Though it does not refer to actual sunlight, it plays with the imagery of light, as does the rest of the gospel of John. It is a testimony to the incarnation of Jesus, and how God dramatically sought to get our attention for all time by becoming a baby. The message of God becoming a baby has been celebrated by us for centuries. It's how God gets our attention. "Hey, I am one of you. I was even a baby. Do you get the point of how much I care for you, for each and every one of you? This baby 'thing' was not easy, but I did it to make a point. Do you get the point?"

Dropped Books

This is an oft-told story, but its relevance for modern day students and its powerful message make it worth including in this collection.

Robert was walking home from school one day when he noticed a boy ahead of him who had dropped all of his books, baseball cap, baseball glove, and laptop computer. Robert came up, knelt down, and helped him pick up all his things. Since there was so much, Robert offered to carry some of the books to the boy's home.

The boy's name was Tom, and he was a new student in the high school where they both attended. Tom was somewhat shy, so Robert did not know his name. Tom was somewhat depressed because he didn't fit in at the high school and some of the other students made fun of him.

When Robert arrived at Tom's house, Tom invited him in for a soda. They talked a little, and Tom appeared to become a little more cheerful. They were both freshmen, so they had a number of things in common to talk about, including girls. After a while Mark went home. But they ate lunch together the next day at school, and they continued to see each other occasionally at school throughout the next four years.

A week before their high school graduation Tom asked Robert to talk with him about something serious. Tom reminded Robert of how he had helped with his books his freshman year, and asked if Robert knw why he had so many books and other things in his arms.

"I cleaned out my locker so as not to leave a mess behind," said Tom. "I planned to go home and commit suicide. I had hidden a number of my mother's opioids from her past surgery, and I was going to take all of them and overdose. But after we spent time together, I realized that you were someone whom I liked. If I killed myself, I realized that I would be missing a potential good friend forever. The years after that proved me correct. So you, Robert, saved my life, when you helped me pick up my books and laptop."

Who could have thought that something so small could have great impact. How many times do we perform an act of kindness, never knowing the ultimate benefits of our actions?

1 John 3:18. "Little children, let us love, not in word or speech, but in truth and action."

Too many young students in high school and college commit suicide. They feel like no one loves them, or they have no future. Sometimes they are bullied to their face or on their computers. What they need are friends and support. For too many, access to opioids is too easy, and it seems to be the method of choice for many teen-age suicides. Easy access to opioids also must be stopped.

Perhaps, the same may describe the experiences of many adults. What we need are more acts of kindness shown to people in our world. Who knows how many suicides may have been stopped simply because someone helped, someone listened, someone cared.

The greater message is that if you show a simple act of kindness to a person, you might be surprised what a significant act of love you may have demonstrated. I was personally told something similar to what Robert heard about an old high school experience of mine. We may never know what are the future results of our kind behavior. Do random acts of love, God is working through you.

The Bishop's Choice

During the Middle Ages a bishop was requested by the pope in Rome to assist the Vatican in making a decision. There were two highly respected priests in north Italian cities whom the pope was considering for possible elevation to the office of bishop. This bishop was asked to make an investigation of the two men to determine which of them would be the more suitable candidate. Both priests were renowned for their piety and their eloquent preaching style.

The bishop thought to himself how important his investigation of these two men would be, so he decided to engage in a special test.

The bishop appeared at the church of the first priest one Sunday morning dressed in the clothing of a beggar. He sat in the back of the church and observed the mass with respect. The ritual and ceremony of the service was grand, the sermon preached by the priest was dramatic and eloquent. After the service, as the priest greeted the members of the parish, the bishop stood to the side not making any movement toward the priest. He wanted to see if the priest would approach him, a stranger and obviously a poor man. The priest made no move. When the members of the parish left, the bishop advanced toward the priest on the steps of the church and spoke. The priest was curt and dismissive toward him. He asked the priest if he could receive some money or food, and he mentioned how he would be willing to work for it. The priest said nothing, but simply went to the rectory.

The next Sunday the bishop appeared at the church of the second priest dressed in the same rags. Likewise, the service was grand and the sermon eloquent. The worshipers were also uplifted by the service. Again, the beggar bishop stood to the side as the priest greeted his own people in the church. But before the disguised bishop could advance toward the priest, the priest came toward him and introduced himself. The priest observed that he was poor and offered him some food at the rectory. The priest took him across the town square to be fed in the priest's quarters. The bishop did not identify himself throughout the entire experience.

Later the bishop reported to the pope his decision concerning the two priests, and the second priest was elevated to the office of bishop. Sometime afterward the bishop went to visit both men in his official attire and explained that it was he who came to them dressed in the form of a beggar, and it was his decision which may have resulted in the decision that was made.

Matthew 25:37-40: (37) Then the righteous will answer him, "Lord, when was it that we saw you hungry and gave you food, or thirsty and

gave you something to drink? (38) And when was it that we saw you a stranger and welcomed, or naked and gave you clothing? (39) And when was it that we saw you sick or in prison and visited you?" (40)

And the king will answer them, "Truly I tell you, just as you did it to one of the least of these who are members of my family you did it to me."

Yes, indeed, the two priests had before themselves someone in rags portraying himself as the least of one of God's creatures. One priest heeded the message of our Lord and attended to the poor people of God; the other priest failed to heed the words of Jesus. He sought rather to feather his own nest of ecclesiastic success in his own parish. How many Christians today see Jesus in the poor, the homeless, and the hungry? I am afraid that too few do. The bishop in our story also knew that too few did in his age, so he undertook the acid test of appearing as one of those poor people in the two churches. It was, I'm sure, a surprise for both priests when they discovered the bishop's ruse. Do we see Jesus in the poor that stand symbolically before us throughout our country and the world? Or are we going to be deceived by God's ruse today?

The Fur Trappers

In the mid nineteenth century there were three fur trappers who worked together in the Rocky Mountains in what is today Colorado. They were successful with trapping through the spring and summer, and they continued trapping into the late fall. They planned to take their furs to the nearest outpost before the winter storms hit, so that they would be safe through the winter season. But their plans went awry when an early blizzard trapped them while they were making the rounds and checking their traps. They began to journey to the nearest outpost in the snowstorm hoping they could make it.

One of the trappers became weakened by the arduous journey and had to be helped along the way by the other two. Finally, one of the trappers said, "We are not going to make it to the outpost, because we are being slowed down by Joe. If all three of us try to make it together, we will all die. We must leave Joe and make it on our own. The other trapper disagreed and refused to leave his friend, Joe. So the first trapper set out in the storm by himself to make it to the outpost at a faster pace. The second trapper continued to move much more slowly because he was burdened with Joe.

The blizzard stopped, and two other trappers, who were friends of the first three men, set out from the outpost in the direction where they knew that their three friends might be found. Along the way they found the first trapper, who had set out on his own. He lay in the snow, frozen to death, a mile from the outpost. Five miles from the outpost they found the other two trappers huddled in the snow. They could no longer travel, but they were still alive. They lay in the snow holding each other tightly. Their body warmth kept both of them alive. They were brought to the outpost where they survived and recovered.

Ruth 1:16: But Ruth said, "Do not press me to leave you or to turn back from following you! Where you go, I will go; where you lodge, I will lodge; your people shall be my people, and your God my God."

In the ancient world the plight of a widow or a single woman alone was horrible; her chances of survival were slim. But these two women committed themselves to each other and increased their chance of survival, and ultimately in the book of Ruth they prevailed with their cooperation. They are like the two fur trappers who saved each other with their body heat. Like Ruth and Naomi, they survived because they stayed together.

Is the fur trapper story also a metaphor for a good marriage? A husband and a wife cling to each other through the challenges of life and they survive. Maybe this story can be told in a wedding sermon? If so, it should be combined with a reading of Genesis 2:24, "Therefore a man leaves his father and his mother and clings to his wife, and they become one flesh." A husband and wife face the vicissitudes of life as the two fur trappers faced the challenge of the storm.

The story is also a parable about any human endeavor. We survive as people in our difficult world when we work together. The lone wolf lives alone and dies alone.

The Cliff

A man was on a camping trip by himself in the Rocky Mountains. He found a beautiful site on a plateau overlooking a valley. He set up his tent for the night and settled in. As it grew dark he began to admire the beauty of the stars, and he wandered away from his campfire. Suddenly, he slipped on soft ground and fell over the edge of the cliff. He fell through vines for a few feet before his hands grasped a few sturdy vines. His fall had stopped and he breathed a sigh of relief. But then a sickening feeling swept over him as he realized his legs were swinging in free air. He was prevented from falling only by his tenacious grip on the few vines looped around his head and upper body. The stars were bright, but there was no moon that night. So as he looked down, he could see only darkness. Since some light did reflect off of the plants around him, it became evident that there was only empty space beneath his feet and potentially a long drop into the valley.

Now he could think. How many elementary rules of camping did he break in order to get into this life threatening situation? He should never have been camping alone. He should not have set his tent up so close to the edge of the plateau. He should not have been wandering around on such a dark night. He should not have wandered so far from his campfire. But it was futile to think of what he should have done, for now he was in this position, and he had to determine how to get out of it. He tried to pull his way up through the vines, but they were green and moist, so that his hands kept slipping back down to the loop of vines which initially broke his fall. He tried to hold onto the vines and walk up the side of the cliff, but the dirt was soft and kept crumbling away. He began to yell, but it was futile, for there was no one to hear. He thought about the possiblity of hanging there until someone found him, but that might take days.

His struggling must have loosen the vines, for he felt himself slipping through the few that had held his upper body. Then he was hanging only the strength of his hands and arms. Soon, he realized, his arms would grow fatigued and he would fall to his death. He thought about his life, and what he had accomplished. He thought about his religious convictions and whether he was ready to face death. He thought about what he believed would happen to him when he died. He prayed to God and finally accepted the inevitability of his own death. Once more he looked into the darkness below, where he could see nothing. How much like life this is, he thought. We know not what lies before us, but we go on living nonetheless. Upon deciding it would be better to face death boldly rather wait for the ultimate fatigue of his arms to passively bring him to his ultimate fate, he said a final prayer and courageously let go. He fell into the darkness below. But he only fell three feet, and then found himself on solid ground, a ledge which jutted out into the darkness unbeknownst to him below the edge of the cliff above. He realized that only when he could accept his death, was life given back to him again.

Psalm 37:5: Commit your way unto the Lord; trust in him, and he will act.

In those moments when we think we are going to die, we sometimes see our whole life in a different and deeper perspective. Flannery O'Connor once had one of her characters say of a woman, "She would have been a good person, if someone would have killed her everyday of her life." When we face the ultimate, we see our lives in clearer fashion.

The parable also talks about letting go and trusting God in matters of life. Sometimes we are afraid to make the big "leap" in our life, the big move, a major decision, and at those times we simply have to let go and let God have our lives. As the Psalmist says, "we must commit our ways unto the Lord" and trust that God will lead us in the right direction.

The Log

Miriam Berg was a widow. Her husband of forty years had died recently and unexpectedly. For years they had lived together and worked in his small, but highly respected bakery, in a small Ukrainian Jewish village in the late nineteenth century. She was heartbroken. She was angry with God for taking her beloved husband from her. After an initial appearance in Friday synagogue services, she stopped coming. The rabbi noticed her absence after about four services, and so he decided to pay her a visit.

It was a cold morning in early winter, and as he walked along the path between the snow piles in the little village, he reflected upon what he might say to her. He approached the neat and well-kept little cottage at the edge of the village, knocked at her door, and waited. Miriam came to the door, silently looked at him, and motioned for him to come in. She was somber and dressed in black, mourning her beloved husband, Jacob the baker. The two of them sat in soft chairs before the fireplace in which a cozy fire burned brightly on that winter morning.

After several minutes of silence on the part of both, a period of time that seemed to last an eternity, the rabbi stood up. He went over to the fireplace and pulled out a small burning log. He placed that burning log on the brick floor that surrounded the fireplace, lest it burn the carpet, of course. He sat back down.

Together they watched the log for some thirty minutes in silence. Slowly the burning log began to burn less brightly until finally the little flames ceased and a small smoldering smoke began to emerge from the log. Eventually the smoke ceased and only a reddish hue appeared on various parts of the log. As the log cooled, even those little reddish hot spots disappeared with the gradual cooling of the log. The rest of the fire still burned brightly, even though Miriam had added no wood.

Miriam never took her eyes off the log. When the last little reddish, glowing spots dimmed to be replaced by the appearance of only dark and burned wood, she spoke.

"Okay, okay, I understand. I will come back to the services next Friday."

Like logs in the fire, we burn brightly and give off light and heat best when we are together. Isolated, we grow cold and fade away.

Ephesians 2:19-22. (19) So then you are no longer strangers and aliens, but you are citizens with the saints and also members of the household of God, (20) built upon the foundation of the apostles and prophets, with Christ Jesus himself as the cornerstone. (21) In him the whole structure is joned together and grows into a holy temple in the Lord; (22) in whom you also are bult together spiritually into a dwelling place for God.

In grand language the author of Ephesians describes the value of belonging to a community of faith. Belonging to such a community meant a great deal for first century Mediterranean Christians. It not only offered them salvation but also gave them a place where they had identity, purpose, and meaning in life, things which so many of them did not have as slaves or women in that oppressive age. We so often fail to appreciate the great spiritual and psychological values we obtain by belonging to a community of faith, a place that provides identity for us. Too many people do not belong to communities of faith, their lives therefore are empty, and they do not know it.

Three Brick Masons

A great cathedral was being build in the south of England, and many good brickmasons and craftsmen were called upon to work on the project. The very special task of carving large stones to be used in the foundational parts of the cathedral was assigned to three very experienced master masons. For several years they plied their craft and the work progressed very well.

One day the chief architect was visiting the site and reviewing the work of all the artisans. He spoke to all three of the master masons concerning their work and its progress,

Upon being asked how he liked the work he did on the cathedral, the first mason said, "It's the greatest challenge of my career. Fortunately, I get paid well, and my family is assured of a good income as long as I keep up this work. I sometimes worry about how long I will be able to keep on this project. But thus far my health is good and I can keep working. I doubt that I'll still be working when the cathedral is finished, but in the meantime, I will put in as much work as possible and get paid nicely for it."

When the second mason was queried concerning his work on the cathedral, he replied, "This is really hard work. But whenever I look up and imagine the finished building, I am impressed by what a great work of art it will be. It will take us years to finish the project, and I don't know if I'll be here when it is done. I hope so. I would like to be remembered as a man who contributed significantly to such a great and noble work of art. I consider myself to be an artist, and I am happy to be part of such a great endeavor."

The architect asked the third mason how he felt about the project, and this was the answer he received: "I am thankful to work on a project that will provide such a beautiful place of worship. People will come here for centuries to worship and praise God, and I am thankful to be able to help make that possible. Each stone must be crafted with care, for the building must last for many generations. Each carefully cut stone is like a hymn offered up to God, and its construction must be worthy of the role it will play in the life of the cathedral in the centuries to come."

Colossians 3:17: And whatever you do, in word or deed, do everything in the name of the Lord Jesus, giving thanks to God the Father through him.

Short words given to us by the author of Colossians, but ever so valuable and meaningful. Live your life with such a positive attitude, and you will live a happy life. See the positive value of your life and work and you will live a satisfying life.

The masons are like people in life. How do you view the road you walk in your journey of life? All three give good answers. The last man sees his life as an act of praise to God. Is he perhaps the happiest of the three? How you view life determines not only your mental health but also your physical health. Do you see the glass as half empty or half full? I so often tell people in my sermons to think about the things that they have, especially in this country, and realize how blessed they are. We take food, water, shelter, and peace for granted, but so many in our world do not have these things. Seeing how much we really have can give us a much more positive attitude about our life in general. Then we can see what we do as having more value and significance.

The Admiral's Ship

The admiral of the fleet was in the lead ship of a small convoy returning to the main port for his fleet. There was a storm which made navigation difficult, but they were moving in the proper direction as best they could, though perhaps a little off course. The admiral's ship spotted a light in the distance, which appeared to be coming closer to them, and it obviously was not part of their convoy. The captain of the lead ship signaled ahead to the source of the light and requested that they move their ship to the port side of his vessel, so that his convoy might pass. The message was sent back that the captain needed to sail his ships to the port side in order to pass safely. The captain had his signalman respond that his was a convoy, and that the single ship up ahead should move to the port side, not him. The message came back, "No, you must move, I cannot move!" At this point the admiral took the place of the captain and ordered the following message flashed ahead, "This is Admiral Hawkes, and I order you to move to port! I am in command of the fleet!" The answer returned. "This is lowly ensign Jones, and I am telling you that you must move your ships to the port side, admiral." There was a pause, while the admiral's anger visibly rose within him, and he responded, "I am an admiral, and I am in command of a fleet." The message returned, "I am an ensign, and I am in command of a lighthouse!" The convoy moved to the port side.

Acts 9:1-6: (1) Meanwhile Saul, still breathing threats and murder against the disciples of the Lord, went to the high priest (2) and asked him for letters to the synagogues at Damascus, so that if he found any who belonged to the Way, men or women, he might bring them bound to Jerusalem. (3) Now as he was going along and approaching Damascus, suddenly a light from heaven flashed around. (4) He fell to the ground and heard a voice saying to him, "Saul, Saul, why do you persecute me?" (5) He asked, "Who are you Lord?" The reply came, "I am Jesus, whom you are persecuting. But get up and enter the city, and you will be told what you are to do."

Saul knew just exactly what he had to do. He had to crush Christians, for they were a heresy and a stain upon Judaism, or at least his interpretation of it. No one more determined than Saul could be found, I suppose. Jesus had to make a special trip and visit him in order to turn him around, and it was a dramatic experience. Once turned around Saul became just as enthusiastic, and perhaps even more, in his advocacy of this new form of Judaism, called the

Way, and ultimately Christianity. But Jesus had to be there like a lighthouse.

Sometimes we are so determined to do that which we think must be done. However, God might have a different plan for us. Listen for the voice of God, and it may be heard in the voices of family, friends, and those around us whose advice sometimes might be best not dismissed. At the turn of the nineteenth century a young British missionary name William Carey was determined to become a missionary to the Islamic world in North Africa, but political events necessitated that he go to India for a time. He was most disappointed, for he knew that his calling was to go to North Africa. Eventually, he spent four decades of his life in India, and gradually came to realize that was where God had wished for him to be in the first place. His significant accomplishments on the mission field have earned him the reputation of being the father of nineteenth century Protestant missionary work in Asia. People propose, but God will ultimately dispose.

The Scratched Diamond

This is another oft-told tale, but it is worth repeating for the value that it has for so many people in our world today. Too often youth despair of themselves and their abilities, but this parable offers a response.

A king once wished to make a beautiful present for his queen, so he decided to give her a beautiful diamond for her birthday. He decided that his present should be special, so he had an uncut diamond purchased in a foreign land and brought to his kingdom. He then hired a master jeweler to cut and shape the diamond for the particular setting he had in mind. The jeweler followed the directions and cut the diamond into the shape that the king desired.

When the jeweler was finished there was a flaw in the face of part of the diamond which he observed as the stone was cut. He brought the diamond to the king and showed him the flaw. The king was so very distraught and said, "Oh, my beautiful diamond is absolutely ruined."

But the jeweler was cautious in responding and finally said, "No, my Lord, I do not believe the diamond is ruined. I merely wished to show you the flaw, so that you would understand why I am going to undertake the next step in preparation."

The king responded, "How can anything you do possibly hide that flaw? It is an ugly scratch or crack, and it is so irregularly shaped. You cannot hide it. You would have to cut the diamond into many smaller diamonds in order to eliminate it. That scratch on the most prominent face of the diamond cannot be hidden."

The jeweler said, "My lord, the diamond is not ruined, but it can be made even more beautiful with this flaw. Trust me, I am a master craftsman."

The king said, "I trust you, but I cannot conceive of how you will hide that crack."

The queen's birthday came, and the jeweler returned to the court with the king's gift wrapped in a beautiful box. The king had not seen what the jeweler had done, so he was quite obviously a little nervous. The jeweler presented the queen with the present, and he said, "Here is a gift, crafted by the request of your husband who loves you very much."

The queen opened the box, while the king waited nervously. She said, "Oh, this is magnificent. This is the most beautiful, precious stone I have ever seen. I will treasure it always."

The king was somewhat surprised. He looked at the stone. Where the flawed crack in the diamond had been, there was now an elegantly etched image of a rose. The irregular crack was superficial enough, so that the jeweler had used it in the design of the rose as the stem and part of one of the petals. The queen continued to speak, and she said to the jeweler, "How ever did you manage to make this diamond so equisite and charming." The king quickly interrupted and said, "It was possible because it was in the hands of the master craftsman."

2 Corinthians 12:9. "My grace is sufficient for you, for power is made perfect in weakness. So, I will boast all the more gladly of my weaknesses, so that the power of Christ may dwell in me."

God has made us all, and so sometimes what we may think is a weakness or shortcoming in ourselves or in others, may really be the source of strength and ability that enables us to do great things. We must attune ourselve to the power of God's grace in our lives, and we may find within us the insight and the ability to use our weaknesses to the greater glory of God and the benefit of the church.

The Rabbi's Journey

This is a nineteenth century Jewish tale told in the Ukraine. Once upon a time there was a very old and wise rabbi who taught young Jewish students to become rabbis. Occasionally he would travel to other villages to speak in the local synagogue. On one such journey he asked a young Jewish student to travel with him. The student was excited to accompany the venerable teacher, for he felt that he could learn a great deal.

After they walked for many hours on the first day, they came to the home of a Jewish farmer, who gave them lodgings for the night. They stayed the night, and in the morning the old rabbi roused the student out of bed to leave. They left quickly without even seeing their host. As they left the house, the student noticed that the farmer's cow was dead and lying in the field. He asked the old rabbi if they could do something. The rabbi said no, for he had prayed that night that the cow would die. The student was aghast that the rabbi would do such a thing to their gracious host.

They came to a village where there was a Jewish community and a synagogue. The rabbi preached a magnificent address that inspired many. After the service several men offered the rabbi and his student lodging for the night. The rabbi accepted the offer of one man and together the host, the rabbi, and his student left. The student overheard several people muttering as to why the rabbi chose the man who was rather notorious for being a somewhat dishonest businessman in the local community. Couldn't the wise old rabbi sense that his host was a shady character? In the morning, the student awoke and the rabbi was not in his bed. The student went outside and found the rabbi plastering a crack in the outside wall of the host's house. The student said to the rabbi that he ought not repair the house of a man who was rich and known to be somewhat dishonest in his dealings. The rabbi silenced him and then said that they must be on their way. Again, they said nothing to their host as they left.

As they arrived in another Jewish village the venerable teacher was received with respect and enthusiasm. He spoke in the synagogue that evening to the delight of the villagers. At the end of the meeting, he was asked to offer up a prayer. So he prayed for the village to be blessed, for their crops to be bountiful, and their families to be healthy. But he ended the prayer with a strange petition that God would bless and keep the czar in his protection. Now Jewish folk had reason to fear and hate the czar of Russia, who so often had oppressed them, even to the point of forbidding the men to have jobs, so that the Jewish wives had to do the work for their families. The folks in the synagogue were puzzled but said nothing.

The venerable rabbi and his student returned home and the student was sullen for a few days. Finally, the old rabbi asked him what was the problem. The student then expressed his concern. How could the old rabbi be so venerable and wise in light of the incident with the dead cow, the plastered wall, and the blessing upon the czar?

"Things are not what they seem, and the ways of the 'Holy One, Blessed Be He' are deep and mysterious at times. When we were at the farmer's home, an angel came to warn me of a demon approaching the home to kill the farmer's only daughter. I prayed that the demon would become confused and his eyes blinded, so that he would kill the cow by mistake. The rich man lives in an old home and there is a treasure hidden away in the stone wall of his house. By patching it, I have ensured that the rich man will never find it. But a century from now a very poor man and his humble family will live there and discover it. I prayed that the czar would be blessed and prosperous. If that happens, he will not bother to tax us poor Jews. I prayed that the 'Holy One' would keep the czar, keep him far away from us. Things are not what they seem to be at first.

Indeed, in our lives we often want something to transpire and we pray for it. When it does not happen, we are disappointed. But then later we discover that what did occur was the better thing for us. God sometimes says no, because in the long run, a better outcome will transpire. Sometimes we pray for things we should not have, we hope for results that best not occur, and we desire that which is not wise for us. Sometimes those events, things, or even people, which we pay little attention to at first turn out to be the most beneficial. The ways of God are mysterious and things are not what they seem at first.

Joseph reassured his brothers in Egypt that he would not seek revenge upon them for selling him into slavery in his youth. He said, "Even though you intended to do harm to me, God intended it for good, in order to preserve a numerous people, as he is doing today" (Gen 50:20). The apparent evil act of the brothers would ultimately save not only their lives, but the lives of countless Egyptians.

FABLES

The following stories are fables or fairy tales. They are sometimes the best narratives for parable story telling. The accounts move in otherworldly time with angels and animals, or sometimes they almost sound historical, but they are on the edge of being unreal.

Nervous Angels

The angels worried. Angels are a rather nervous lot to begin with; they tend to flutter around a lot and leave feathers here and there. Oh yes, they have power, they put up a good fight with demons, but then demons aren't really good fighters either. Angels can be sweet and charming, and sometimes they get painted to look like babies because they're so cute. They are just angels, of course. When God shared his plans with them, they just went ballistic. What God planned to do was just too dangerous.

God loved people and wanted to demonstrate in the most dramatic way possible that he loved them. God hoped that by this demonstration of divine love, people would be inspired to love each other. The angels were skeptical; they didn't think that people could really be inspired to be noble or loving. The angels studied human history a little too much; it made them pessimistic. They believed that God should start over with the porpoises; they had said that ever since Cain killed Abel and invented murder and war. But God was determined. God was always so hopeful. God told the angels that he was going to become a human being and live on earth to teach people to be loving, and then he would demonstrate the ultimate act of love for them. The angels were impressed.

The angels, of course, expected that God would go down and become a great philosopher, perhaps in Athens, where great philosophers abounded. Or perhaps God would become a great lawgiver and take up residence in Rome. He would issue great laws in Rome, but, of course, such Roman justice never extended to the peoples they conquered. Perhaps God would change that by becoming a great legal reformer in Rome and extending justice to everyone in the Roman Empire. Perhaps God would become a great priest in Persia and work within the monotheistic religion of Zoroastrianism. The angels were interested.

When they heard that God had chosen to be a Jew, their little angel jaws dropped and a few feathers fluttered to the floor. The Jews had glory days in the past under David, but those days were gone. Now Jews were simply a lowly little province, most recently crushed in a futile rebellion. "Why the Jews?" they said. God told them that he wished to identify with poor people. That way people everywhere and in all times would take his message seriously if he identified with the lowly.

Then God told them that he would not appear as a fully grown adult, but he would do the entire human life span, he would begin as a baby.

The eyes of many of the angels began to twitch nervously. Some of the angels wailed. "Do you know what mortality rates are for babies," they asked, "especially in poor countries?" They further lamented, "Over half of them never make it to adulthood." They composed themselves and said, "Well, I suppose if you were born in one of the royal palaces to a Herodian queen, that would be okay!"

God told them that he had chosen a fourteen-year-old peasant girl for a mother and an older retired carpenter for a father.

Angels fluttered everywhere screaming insanely, "No, no, no, no, you can't do that!"

But God quietly said, "I need to show all human beings that I love them. Most of them throughout history are poor peasants like the two that I have chosen for parents. What does it say, if I take the easy way, and get born of rich and powerful parents? If my message is to gain attention, it must be because of the power of the message itself, not because I had such a head start in life. I want people to love each other, so I have to show them serious love by my own actions. I will be born a baby to poor parents in a poverty stricken country in a horrible age. That way I can get my point across."

"Where do you intend to be born?" one angel asked.

God responded, "In a stable, in a manger, while my parents are on a trip and cannot afford good accommodations."

Now the angels were so stunned, they could not utter a word. But you could see their angel wings quivering. God continued, "And I don't want to see any of you showing up to clean up the stable."

"But …….. but …….. but …….," they said, "We need to do something."

God said, "You can come down and sing."

"Oh good, we can do that," they replied, "to whom will we sing?"

"Shepherds," God said.

"Shepherds, like the kind that live with sheep? Don't you mean metaphorical shepherds, like kings and the like?"

"No," said God, "I mean shepherds . . . sheep . . . . wool . . . mutton. You know . . ."

"But shepherds don't appreciate good music; we might as well send down a twentieth century rock band," moaned the angels.

"Practice your music," said God. "Oh yes, and select one of your number to announce to those shepherds that I am being born in a nearby stable."

By this time the angels were howling their disapproval. Feathers from their wings were falling all over the floors of heaven. God had to silence them, "Gabriel, Michael, Uriel, Muriel, Kim, Betsy, Tiffany, Tanisha, Ivonna, Sheneeka, be quiet!" (You figure that if everyone has at least one guardian angel, and some of us need more, there must be more names for them than there are people on earth.)

One of the angels asked about that special sign that God said he was going to undertake.

"Well, I intend to suffer and die on a cross, crucified by Roman soldiers, and then rise from the dead a couple of days later."

Five million or so angels fainted. It was quite the scene. But God was undeterred, and he decided to do it.

"Oh yeah," said God, "one or two of you can announce my resurrection from the tomb on Sunday."

Luke 2:8-14: (8) In that region there were shepherds living in the fields, keeping watch over their flock by night. (9) Then an angel of the Lord stood before them, and the glory of the Lord shone around them, and they were terrified. (10) But the angel said to them, "Do no be afraid; for see—I am bringing you good news of great joy for all the people: (11) to you is born this day in the city of David a Savior, who is the Messiah, the Lord. (12) This will be a sign for you: you will find a child wrapped in bands of cloth and lying in a manger." (13) And suddenly there was with the angel a multitude of the heavenly host, praising God and saying, (14) "Glory to God in the highest heaven, and on earth peace among those whom he favors!"

We celebrate Christmas and Easter so often, that we sometimes fail to hear the incredible drama that occurs in this story. That is what we celebrate on Christmas eve. Our God has done great things for us. He shocked the angels. Does it grab our attention? Can we understand? Can we respond? Can we show the love he sought to inspire? Gather around the manger and say, "What great love is this."

The Rainman

In the early days of the Spanish settlement of the southwest there was a little village that suffered from drought. The villagers heard of a great rainmaker who could bring rain to the driest fields and cause them to produce great yield. So they sent for the rainmaker to come to their village and save them from drought and starvation. He arrived one Saturday and then immediately began to discuss with the villagers when he would work his magic to bring them the rain they needed so badly.

"What about Sunday," he said, for he realized how badly they needed rain, so he suggested that he begin to work his magic the very next day.

"Not on Sunday," said the villagers, "for that is the day we wear our finest clothing to church, and in the afternoon we stroll about on the town square and talk to all our friends. If it rains on Sunday, our finest clothes will be ruined, and our day of rest and congeniality will be spoiled."

The rainmaker then suggested Monday. "Oh no, not on Monday," they said, "for on Monday all the women to do their washing, and they hang their laundry out to dry. If it rains, all the laundry will remain wet and perhaps even begin to mildew. We cannot do it on Monday."

"Then let me suggest Tuesday," replied the rainmaker.

"Well, this Tuesday is very special," said the villagers. "Don Hernandez's daughter is to be married in the village church, and there will be a grand reception on the town square. It would be a shame to ruin such a fine wedding, as we know that Don Hernandez will provide such for the village. We will be dancing in the streets for the wedding reception, and we cannot dance in the mud that the rain will create with the dry dust."

"Is Wednesday an acceptable day," quipped the rainmaker, who was becoming somewhat impatient with the villagers.

"Not exactly," they said. "On Wednesday the cattlemen come to town, and they bring their cattle through the streets to the pens at the end of the city. If there is rain, the cattle will trample through muddy streets and make a very bad mess of our city and tear up the dirt streets. It will be very difficult to clean up muddy streets especially if there are cow droppings mixed in with the mud. Dry streets are much easier to clean after the cattle pass."

Is there a possibility that Thursday might be a good day for a rainstorm for at least a few minutes," said the rainmaker in rather sarcastic fashion.

"Oh no, no," said the villagers, "for that is the holy day of the patron saint of our parish. We will have a special service in her honor with a festive parade through the city after the service. We do not want to spoil our very special festival day. We cannot parade in the rain and hold her statue high in the procession. The rain may damage the statue. Nor do we want to parade in the rain and the mud with our fine clothing."

"Well then," said the exasperated rainmaker, "Before I even ask, tell me why Friday is not a good day either."

The villagers sheepishly said, "Well, actually, this coming Friday is the day when the men of the village finally planned to do major repairs on the town meeting center and some of the other buildings in the town square. It would be best if they had good weather on that day, so that they might finish their work that we have been anticipating for some time now. If they do roof repair, then the rain will fall into the rooms of the buildings and cause damage."

By this point the rainmaker could see that it was going to be very difficult to schedule an immediate date for the villagers. So he said, "I will return next Saturday." By that time I want you to choose a day next week when I can definitely bring rain. Meet together with each other and resolve your scheduling difficulties. I expect you to have a firm date when I return."

True to his word the rainmaker came that next Saturday. But when he arrived, there was no village to be found. The drought had become so bad that everything in the village dried up and blew away—houses, trees, people, dogs, cattle, everything. He looked around and realized there was nothing to be saved by bringing rain. All he could see was sagebrush blowing in the wind. For the village, and its people and all the objects in it, had dried up and turned into sagebrush blowing around in the dry, arid wind.

That is where sagebrush in the southwest comes from, and it still blows around with no place to fix itself. It came from that little village that could not make up its mind. For just as the people could not fix a date for the rainmaker, so the sagebrush can never fix itself permanently to the ground.

Never put off until tomorrow, what you can do today.

Proverbs 27:1: Do not boast about tomorrow, for you do not know what a day may bring.

James 4:13: Yet you do not even know what tomorrow will bring. What is your life? For you are a mist that appears for a little while and then vanishes.

All of the people in the little village could not focus upon what was truly important, ending the drought. All the mundane regular things of their community life were more important, so they delayed the bringing of the rain. Do what is important now. They didn't, and thus, they died. As James 4:13 implies, focus upon what is important, for life can be fleeting. The story also has another level of meaning. See what is important in your life and don't get lost in details. See the value of family, friends, relationships, and your religious and spiritual life; do not focus on the short-term goals, worries, and agenda of everyday life to the exclusion of the former.

The Fourth Wise Man

Not many folk know that there actually was a fourth wise man who accompanied his more famous companions to visit that baby Christ child so long ago. We all know of Caspar, Melchior, and Balthazar with their gold, frankincense and myrrh, but of that fourth wise man we know little. In his piety he desired to bring the baby Jesus electrum, a special mixture of gold and silver, that in the minds of some people was more valuable than either gold or silver by themselves.

The four wise men came from diverse realms and met together as some exotic location forever lost to our memory. They then followed that famous star of Bethlehem as "it" or "he" led them, for it may have been an angel. The "star" hung low in the sky and led them toward the holy land; finally the "star" hovered over the dwelling where the Christ child was to be found (sounds like an angel to me).

As they traversed the wilderness, they traveled through one of those nameless villages that are found in the nooks and crannies of the ancient Near East. They stopped for water for themselves and their camels and moved onward. But the fourth wise man noticed the gaunt appearance of some of the villagers. He asked and discerned that a famine had afflicted the village because locusts had eaten the grain crop the previous harvest season. He was so moved by the sight of their frail bodies, especially those of the children, he determined to do something. He parted ways with the other three wise men and went to a neighboring village not afflicted by the famine and there purchased a great quantity of food with his extremely valuable electrum. Returning with the food, he provided the villagers with sufficient supplies to last them through to the next harvest season. But now he had no gift to bring to the Christ child. He returned home and firmly decided that he would come at a later time to find the Christ child.

Ten years later he set forth on another journey with more electrum to give as a gift to the young boy Jesus. He traveled alone this time. As he neared the holy land he found himself near an encampment of people. He discovered that they were ill with some disease that they may have gotten from eating bad food or drinking bad water. They needed some medical attention. So he rode to the nearest village and obtained simple medical supplies and a doctor to return to the encampment. There were quite a few sick people and so the supplies and doctor's services required that he spend all of his electrum. Again, he was without a gift for the young Jesus. He returned home and promised to make the long journey a third time.

Twenty years later he came back to Palestine with his gift of electrum. This time he decided not to head to Galilee where Jesus lived, but to go to Jerusalem, for as he drew near to Palestine, he heard that Jesus was teaching in Jerusalem. As he neared Jerusalem he encountered a band of people who had been seized by Herod's soldiers because they had not paid their debts. They were to be sold as debt slaves. His heart went out to them, especially because there were so many children in their number. Once more he used the electrum to pay the debts, and once more he had no gift for Jesus.

But this time he decided to journey on to Jerusalem without a gift. After thirty years he was determined to at least see Jesus. As he approached the city of Jerusalem, he encountered some women who were crying bitterly. Upon asking them why they were so sorrowful, they replied that the great teacher from Galilee had been crucified by the Romans that afternoon. The wise man realized with horror that they were talking about Jesus. He had failed. Not only had he not delivered a gift to Jesus, he had failed completely to see Jesus on any of his three trips. He was a failure.

He remained in Jerusalem for two days before beginning the long journey back home. As he saddled his camel and began to sadly traverse the desolate stretch of land east of Jerusalem to the Jordan River, he suddenty encountered a bright light before him in the road. As his eyes adjusted, he realized that he was seeing Jesus. Though he had never seen him in real life, he knew that this was Jesus appearing to him. He jumped down off of his camel and began to profusely apologize. He said, "I am so sorry I was not able to bring you a gift when you were born, or in any of the years after that. I tried three times, but I failed to reach you every time."

From the glowing light before him a voice came. "You did not fail. You were the most successful of all the wise men. You brought me a gift three times, wonderful gifts, gifts of love. When you fed the hungry, healed the sick, and freed the slaves, you were doing that to me. Yours were the greatest gifts that could be given." Stunned by this message, the fourth wise man began to cry, but not tears of sorrow, rather tears of joy. The glowing light disappeared, the fourth wise man mounted his camel and continued his journey. He was at last satisfied. He had brought his gift to the Christ child.

Matthew 2:9-12: (9) When they had heard the king, they set out; and there, ahead of them, went the star that they had seen at its rising, until it stopped over the place where the child was. (10) When they saw that the star had stopped, they were overwhelmed with joy. (11) On entering the house, they saw the child with Mary his mother; and they knelt down and paid him homage. Then, opening their treasure chests, they offered him gifts of gold, frankincense, and myrrh. (12) And having been warned in a dream not to return to Herod, they left for their own country by another road.

The wise men were led to baby Jesus by a star, which is obviously an angel, which is why we put either a star or an angel atop our Christmas trees. Then they went home. We never hear from them again. It is romantic to suggest that was not the end of the story and that perhaps there was a fourth magus. Matthew's point was that even the foreign magicians pay homage to Jesus, and that occurs even before his birth. But it is fun to envision an addition to the story with another significant point—that homage to the poor is also homage to Jesus. Helping babes around the world who lack clean water, food, clothing, and shelter is indeed bringing a gift to baby Jesus.

When I was a Cub Scout in the 1950s I used to read *Boy's Life*, the scout magazine. One fictional story told of space travelers who went from planet to planet trying to find Jesus as he appeared in each world. In their most recent attempt they landed on a planet and came to a holy city just after he had been crucified, just as had happened on the previous planets they visited. Jesus was for them so elusive, and yet they could have found him on planet Earth among the poor.

The Rabbi's Prayer

Once there was a rabbi who served a small, isolated Jewish village two centuries after the time of Jesus. The village was struck by plague and the poor villagers came to the rabbi and said, "Rabbi, pray to the Holy One, Blessed be He, that He might take away the plague." So the rabbi searched his sacred texts and found the solution. At dusk he was to go into the woods and find a great oak tree where he would offer up a special prayer that would end the plague. He did so, and the plague ceased. The villagers rejoiced and thanked God.

A generation later plague again struck the village, and the villagers went to the rabbi for help. "Rabbi, pray to the Holy One, Blessed be He, that He might take away the plague," they cried. He was a new rabbi, but he knew what his predecessor had done to end the plague many years prior. He looked through the records of his predecessor and learned of the prayer and the oak tree. So he went into the woods at dusk with the prayer, but the oak tree was gone. So he prayed the prayer in an open field at dusk. The plague ended, and the villagers rejoiced and thanked God.

Another generation passed, and again a plague afflicted the village. The villagers cried, "Rabbi, pray to the Holy One, Blessed be He, that He might take away the plague." This rabbi knew about the deeds of his two predecessors. He read their old records, but he could not determine what time of day he should offer the petition because the texts were so worn. So he went early in the morning. The oak tree was gone, the time was wrong, but he had the correct prayer. He prayed and the plague ended. Again the villagers rejoiced and thanked God.

Finally, another generation passed and another plague struck the village. Yet again the villagers went to the rabbi and cried, "Rabbi, pray to the Holy One, Blessed be He, that He might take away the plague." The new rabbi read the old records and could not determine what prayer had been used. So he did not know the prayer, nor the time of day, and the oak tree was gone. But he went into the woods at noon and prayer a brief prayer from his heart, "O Holy One, if it be your will, deliver your poor people from this affliction." The plague ended.

Psalm 120:1: In my distress I cry to the Lord, that he may answer me.

The initial point to be made is that God answered the prayer of four rabbis in four different generatons praying that the plague might be ended. God heard, God answered. The faith of the petitioner was vindicated. Pray to the Lord in distress.

Bt there is also another message in the text that is evident in the overall plot line. Increasingly the rabbis lack what they need to make an effective prayer, but in each instance a gracious deity responds to their heartfelt prayers despite the inadequacies of their petitionary process. The heartful prayer was sufficient.

It is an understood Jewish principle: If you have the rules, follow them; if you don't have guidelines, use your common sense, God will understand. This story taken from an ancient collection of Jewish tales called the *Pirke Aboth*, "Tales of the Fathers," indicates to us that the ancient rabbis were not legalists. They often felt that moral behavior was a mark of common sense more than a strict observation of the traditions. If you have the rules, follow them as an act of praise and devotion, if you lack the rules, do what you believe to be right. Christians, too, need to be reminded that in many instances of moral behavior and church life God would have us use the common sense that was imparted to us by the Creator rather than slavishly following our own rules, ecclesiatical guidelines, or old traditions.

The Fool on the Fence

Outside the great city a fool sat on a fence. The great road from the city passed by this fence, so that every day the people who left the city to go to their homes passed by this fool. They observed the fool sitting on the fence every day.

I do not know when the custom began, perhaps in the distant, distant past. Individuals or groups would go up to the fool and look into his face. His dull eyes showed no recognition and he avoided gazing into any person's eyes. They could sense he was of low intelligence. They would place on one side of the fool a nickel, and on the other side a dime. They would say to the fool, "Fool, choose the greater of the two coins!"

The fool would look at the little shiny dime and then the big fat nickel. Again, he would look at the dime and then the nickel. Then he would grab the nickel and giggle. He would hold the nickel tightly and rock back and forth on the fence. The people would laugh, and the fool would then laugh even more. People would say, "Oh silly fool, oh foolish fool. You always choose the nickel." The fool would hold his nickel and look at them blankly. They would walk away laughing. This little scenario was repeated many times daily for perhaps many years.

One day the great Wise Man came forth from the city. He observed this little game played out several times. Finally, he had to speak. He went up to the fool and said, "Fool, fool, will you never learn? Every day you choose the nickel time and time again. Will you never learn from the laughter of the crowd that you have chosen wrongly? Though the nickel is bigger than the dime, it is worth only half as much. Why do you keep making this mistake?"

Suddenly the fool's eyes brightened as he looked straight into the Wise Man's eyes. With a subtle expression on his face, the fool said, "You may indeed speak the truth, O wise man. The dime may be worth more than the nickel. But I know this. Were I to choose the dime but once, I would never be offered choice of nickel or dime again. As is, I have nickels aplenty every day, for the rest of my life."

1 Corinthians 4:10. "We are fools for the sake of Christ, but you are wise in Christ."

Who is wise and who is foolish in our world? The fool on the fence sees what others perhaps do not see. St. Paul speaks of how the world adjudges Christians to be fools for their belief in Jesus. But like the fool on the fence they see what others do not. They see by faith and not by reason. The wise man's reason declares Christians to be fools. But by faith Christians see what others cannot, a loving God who cares for them. Who then is wise and who is foolish? Christians are foolish by the standards of the world, but they are wise in the eyes of God. The fool sits on the fence and sees into the sky, the rest rush hurriedly on their way perhaps looking only at the ground.

Killer Watermelons

There was a village of simple folk who lived in a mountain valley far from the rest of the towns and villages in their country. They were good but naïve people. So it was not surprising that when some watermelons began growing not too far from their village, they did not know what these plants were. Who planted the water-melons, I supppose, we will never know. At any rate, the villagers grew fearful of thse strange objects that grew so large. They suspected that the watermelons posed a threat to their village, so they sent a message to the king of their land asking for help.

The king sent a messenger to explain to the villagers that the watermelons were not dangerous, but rather they were edible plants, and quite enjoyable at that. The messenger gathered the people in the town square and began to explain to them what kind of fruit the watermelons were, and how they could be grown and eaten. The villagers did not understand his learned explanations about fruit, and they were suspicious about this stranger whom they did not know. They suspected that he intended to lead them out into a trap to be ambushed by the watermelons. So they did not listen to his explanations, and he returned to the king somewhat irritated by their response.

So the king sent another messenger. He brought watermelons in a bag into their village. He, too, told the people that the watermelons were not fierce beasts, but rather harmless fruits. He then pulled a watermelon out of the bag, cut it into four parts, and began to eat some of the watermelon. This truly terrified the people. "Oh no!" they said. "Now the horrible watermelons will take revenge on our city because we have killed and eaten one of them." So they drove the messenger out of the village, so that the watermelons would know that they had nothing to do with the murder of one of their watermelon family.

A third messenger was sent to them by the king. He decided to play along with the fear of the villagers. He came and said that indeed the watermelons were dangerous and needed to be dealt with. The villagers trusted him at first because he reinforced their fears and told them what they suspected all along. He then led them out to a hill overlooking the watermelon patch. As they gazed at the patch, he suddenly ran down the hill screaming, drew forth a sword, and began chopping up watermelons. Before their very eyes he began to devour the watermelons. This man, who could charge directly into the nest of the dreaded watermelons and destroy them so violently, must be an even worse beast than the watermelons themselves. So they ran in fear from the messenger whenever he tried to approach them again.

A fourth messenger came to the people. But he did not tell them that he was a messenger sent from the king. Rather, he came as a simple peasant looking for work in their village. He told them that he shared their fear of watermelons, and that he would not venture near the watermelons himself. After working in their midst for a year, he gained their trust. One day he said he was going out to observe the watermelons for several hours. The next day when he went out to the watermelon patch, several villagers went with him to observe the motionless watermelons for several hours. After that he would creep up and touch the watermelons and sit with them, while the other villagers observed him. Eventually the other villagers did the same thing as he. Gradually the villagers began to recognize that indeed the watermelons were simply plants, and slowly the messenger taught them how to cut and eat the watermelons. But as he did this, he always acted as though it was a great act of discovery for himself as well as for them. In time the village not only grew to love its watermelon patch, but they became very wealthy by their ability to sell watermelons throughout the kingdom.

1 Corinthians 9:19-22: (19) For though I am free with respect to all, I have made myself a slave to all, so that I might win more of them. (20) To the Jews I became as a Jew, in order to win Jews. To those under the law I became as one under the law (though I myself am not under the law) so that I might win those under the law. (21) To those outside the law I became as one outside the law (though I am not free from God's law but am under Christ's law) so that I might win those outside the law. (22) To the weak I became weak, so that I might win the weak. I have become all things to all people, that I might by all means save some.

Paul describes exactly what the fourth servant did: he became a simple peasant in order to win their trust and gradually accomplish a successful resolution to the watermelon crisis. The parable speaks of patience with people in bringing them to the truth of the message of the Gospel. In general, the parable speaks of patience in all of our dealings with people. It also provides good advice to clergy in how to deal with members of their congregations and move them forward.

Spear in the Air

The animals of the jungle gathered together in a meeting called by the king of beasts, the old lion. He told them that he was old and tired, and it was time for a new king to be chosen. The new animal to be chosen, however, would have to pass a test. The nature of the test would be as follows: a spear would have to be thrown into the air. While it was in the air, the animal would count to twenty, and the count had to be complete before the spear touched the ground. The animals all agreed that this would be a fair test of someone who should succeed the lion. For it would take strength to throw the spear high enough, and it would take at least some intelligence to count to twenty correctly. A lot of animals did not try for that reason.

Up stepped the giraffe. Everyone said, "Oh, he should have a good chance to pass the test. For he already is so tall, that the spear will be thrown high into the air, and that will give him time to count to twenty."

The giraffe threw the spear, and it went high into the air. But as he started to count the words got caught in his long, long throat, and they were slow to come out. The spear struck the ground, and he had only gotten to eight.

Next came the hippopotamus. Evryone said, "Oh, he is so strong. Surely, he will throw the spear higher into the air than the giraffe, and that will give him time to count to twenty."

The hippopotamus indeed threw the spear higher than any of the other animals could. But despite its height in the air and the fast counting by the hippopotamus, the spear still struck the ground before he could reach twenty. He got to sixteen. The animals realized that if the strength of the hippopotamus could not throw the spear high enough, perhaps none of them could pass the test.

The cheetah stood up and said, "I see that we must add something to the task in addition to brute strength." So the cheetah ran across the plain with tremendous speed, and as he ran up the side of a small hill, he threw the spear with all the strength and momentum he could muster. The momentum carried over to the spear as it sailed high into the sky. It went very high, even higher than the throw of the hippopotamus. He might have even been able to count to twenty, except that he was out of breath from running so furiously across the plain. He got to thirteen.

Then the chimpanzee stepped up to throw the spear. All the animals laughed at him. "You are too weak to throw the spear high enough," they said. "You are very smart," said the animals, "but this test requires strength. Maybe more strength than any of us have."

The chimpanzee took the spear, looked to the lion for approval to try, and the lion nodded. The chimpanzee threw the spear up into the air, but it did not go very high at all. But he counted, "five, ten, fifteen, twenty." He reached twenty before the spear struck the ground. He then looked to the lion, and said, "You never said that we had to count to twenty by ones, so I counted by fives."

The lion nodded and said, "Not always does strength mean that you are fit to rule, sometimes wisdom is the best virtue." So the monkey succeeded the lion as king of beasts in the jungle.

Matthew 10:16: "See, I am sending you out like sheep into the midst of wolves; so be wise as serpents and innocent as doves."

The chimpanzee came forward and was respectful and meek. But the chimpanzee was also very smart to count by fives when he undertook the test. This is an example of what Jesus calls for from his disciples. Be meek and respectful, but use your common sense and be clever in the world. Don't cheat, but be clever. This is how Christians can succeed in spreading the kingdom of God. This is how individual congregations can survive and succeed in our modern world. This is how Christian individuals can live in the world around them.

Wine and the Country Doctor

In a small French village in the heart of the wine producing part of the country, a country doctor faithfully served the villagers for many years, healing their illnesses, delivering babies, providing vaccinations, and patiently listening to their health complaints. Often the poorer villagers could not pay him, so he provided his services free. Thus, he was somewhat poor himself.

When it came time for him to retire, the villagers decided that they should honor him for his many years of service. A special gift, reflective of the personality of the community, should be their precious offering. They would provide him with a large vat of wine, which he could sell to obtain some retirement income. Each little villager, the head of each family, would bring forth a ten gallon container of wine to pour into the large vat in the center of the village as part of a special ceremony to honor the doctor. Thus, their gift would come from the labor of their hands and from their vineyards, for which they were famous.

One vineyardman, Pierre, thought to himself, "The doctor sure has been good to me and my family over the years. But ten gallons of wine is a lot for me to provide, and the expense will be difficult on my small income. . . . I know what I will do. I will go down to the creek and fill my ten gallon container with fresh springwater. A little springwater mixed in with all that other wine will not be noticed. The good doctor will not notice. And it will certainly help me and my family by saving the expense of ten gallons of wine." So that is what Pierre did.

The day of the retirement celebration arrived. The village had a small parade down the center of the town, the mayor gave a grand speech, as mayors are prone to do, and they then turned their attention to the large vat in the town square.

The head of each family stood in line with his ten gallon container, and one by one they poured the contents of their container into the large vat. Because each container had a spout to pour into the spout of the vat, one could not see the wine as it was poured. Pierre knew that this would be the process, so he was sure he could pour his spring water into the vat, and no one could see that it was water. As he stood in line, he felt a little guilty, but he steeled himself, knowing that he did what was necessary for his financial situation.

Finally, each of the vineyardmen emptied the contents of his container. The mayor stepped forward and with a flourish gave a ladle to the country doctor. The doctor then dipped the ladle into the opening atop the vat and drew forth the contents of the vat. He raised the ladle to his lips and tasted the gift of the villagers, their gift of love to him for his many years of service. He tasted their gift, and he tasted the purest, freshest springwater imaginable. For it seems that all the little villagers went down to the creek and filled their ten gallon containers with springwater.

Proverbs 20:6: "Many proclaim themselves loyal, but who can find one worthy of trust?"

Such is the way of the world in showing love and respect to people. The way of the world is to give a parade and fancy speeches, but its acts of love are ever so shallow, so hallow, so empty, so fake. They are done in self-serving fashion. The true love of Christians by comparison is real and meaningful, or so it should be. Many people will declare themslves to be your friends, but in difficult times, they disappear. They will slap you on the back and declare their faithfulness to you, but in time of distress, they will disappear. A Christian will be loyal to his or her friends in time of difficulty and not simply disappear.

The Father's Palace

A man received a letter from a distant country telling him that his father, whom he had hardly known, had died. The letter further informed him that he had inherited his father's palace, and that all he needed to do was come and claim his possession. So the man packed his bags and journeyed to that distant land.

Upon arriving at the palace, he found a guard in front of the palace entrance. He then said to the guard, "My father has died and has left me this palace. Will you grant me permission to enter the palace of my father?"

The guard replied, "I cannot at this time grant you permission to enter the palace of your father." So the man sat down and waited several days outside the palace.

He then arose and asked the guard, "Can you now grant me permission to enter the palace of my father?" He felt that certainly the guard would give him permission after he had patiently waited several days in the presence of the man.

The guard replied, "I still cannot give you permission to enter the palace of your father." The man then sat down and waited several years in the presence of the guard.

Finally, he arose and asked the guard the question again, "Can you *now* grant me permission to enter the palace of my father?" For he had waited years outside the palace in the presence of the guard.

Again, the guard responded, "No! I still cannot grant you permission to enter your father's palace." The man once more sat down and waited.

He waited many years, until he was so old that he could no longer move. He was close to death. He motioned the guard to come over to him, and he asked in a weakened voice, "When would you have given me permission to enter the palace of my father?"

The guard then said, "I could never have given you permission to enter your father's palace! It was never in my authority to grant you that permission. It was your right to enter the palace at any time you wished. For the palace belonged to you, not to me. I am merely your guard. I cannot give you permission to enter your palace." Upon hearing that, the man then died without ever having entered the palace of his father. What was his to freely take, he never took.

John 8:36. "So if the Son makes you free, you will be free indeed."

These simple words are often hard for people to realize in the depths of their being. The message of God is that we are freely forgiven, we do not have to work to earn our salvation. The kingdom of God is ours, the castle of our Father can be entered freely. Yet too many in guilt or fear cannot accept this free gift. God forgives us, but sometimes it is harder for us to forgive ourselves. This is an excellent Reformation story.

Some Christians speak of a conversion experience and coming to Jesus. I don't know whether I would say that they had a conversion experience and became Christians for the first time. Some times Christians will realize to the depth of their being what the message of Jesus is about, and though they've heard all their lives, they just took it for granted. Then it dawns on them that they are truly forgiven, accepted, and loved in the eyes of God, and they really don't do anything to deserve it. Some people have this experience several times in their lives. It is an amazing message and really should strike us in a dramatic fashion when we think about the message in its deepest meaning.

Just Little Birds

A great heat wave swept across the Serengeti plain in Africa bringing a great drought. All the animals met together and discussed what plans they might make to drive away the heat wave. The lions suggested that they, as the most regal of all beasts, use their mighty power and roar at the sun to make it disappear behind the clouds, and thus bring rain. And so they they did. They roared and roared. They roared until they became hoarse, and nothing happened. The elephants came forward with pomposity and proposed spraying water into the air in order to create a small rainstorm which might attract more rain. So they drew what little water was left from the watering hole and sprayed it into the air from their trunks. It fell to the ground and upon the other animals, but alas, nothing happened. The monkeys believed themselves to be the smartest of all the creatures (and their relatives, human beings, brashly seem to think the same thing incorrectly about themselves). So they decided to form committees to arrive at some guidelines for action and possible solutions. They set to chattering in their committees, and of course, like human parliaments and Congress, they accomplished nothing. They continued to chatter throughout the rest of the parable. Finally, the small birds came forward with an idea. But before they could speak, all the other animals began to laugh at them. For how could such small and seemingly insignificant creatures accomplish anything? But not to be dissuaded, the birds set off on their own to solve the problem. They flew together in great numbers up into the sky. They flew close to the sun and blocked the hot rays coming from the sun. With the earth shaded, the temperature cooled, and soon rain came to the parched earth. The other animals stood in amazement. For such little creatures were able to accomplish what great creatures had failed to do. For such is the nature of determination in both people and animals in times of great difficulty. Little folk, when well organized and working as a team, may accomplish great things.

1 Samuel 17:33, 42-43, 49: (33) Saul said to David, "You are not able to go against this Philistine to fight with him; for you are just a boy, and he has been a warrior from his youth." . . . (42) When the Philistine looked and saw David, he disdained him, for he was only a youth, ruddy and handsome in appearance. (43) The Philistine said to David, "Am I a dog, that you come to me with sticks?" . . . (49) David put his hand in his bag, took out a stone, slung it, and struck the Philistine on his forehead; the stone sank into his forehead, and he fell face down on the ground.

Never underestimate someone because of their size or their youth. Never underestimate what you can do either. In Indianapolis, Indiana a number of years ago, a thirteen-year-old girl in a Roman Catholic church heard about the plight of Cambodian children who lost legs because they stepped on land mines left over from the Viet Nam war in the 1970s. She proposed that the church youth attempt to purchase prosthetic limbs for some of these children. People told her it was an impoossible and expensive undertaking for someone so young as she was. But she organized the youth of her school and church to have candy sales, bake sales, car washes, and other humble projects. After one year they presented their first prosthetics to a young Cambodian teenager, who was a refugee in America. Do not say, I am too young, too old, too poor, too weak, or too anything to serve in the kingdom of God!

The Cracked Pot

In India a water carrier had two large pots, hanging on opposite ends of a long pole which he carried on his shoulders. One of the pots was cracked and leaked water, but the water carrier used it anyway. The other pot was intact and always delivered the full portion of water from the stream up to the house where the man lived. The cracked pot usually only delivered half of its original contents to the house, and it lost water all the way up the little path trod by the water carrier.

For three years the water carrier thus carried a pot and a half of water to his home every day. The intact pot was proud of its contribution to the life of the man, but the cracked pot was deeply ashamed of its imperfection, and sad that it could only accomplish half of its assigned task.

One day the cracked pot spoke to the water carrier, saying, "I am so sorry and ashamed of what I do. Please forgive me and replace me."

"Why?" said the water carrier.

"Every day I lose half of the water that you put into me before we reach your home. Because of my crack, your labors are wasted as the water is lost. You do this work for nothing."

The water carrier said to the poor cracked pot, "As we return to my house, I want you to notice the beautiful flowers along the narrow path we walk."

As they climbed the hill the cracked pot saw the beautiful wild flowers on his side of the path, which did not exist on the other side.

At the top of the hill, the water carrier said to the cracked pot, "Did you notice the flowers on your side of the path, but that there were no flowers on the other side of the path? I have always known about your flaw, but I put it to good use. As we walked up the hill, the water you leaked out, watered those beautiful flowers. The flowers flourished. I picked them and gave them to my wife and decorated our table with them. Without you I could never have enjoyed those beautiful flowers."

Romans 12:4-8: (4) For as in one body we have many members, and not all the members have the same function, (5) so we, who are many, are one body in Christ, and individually we are members one of another. (6) We have gifts that differ according to the grace given to us; prophecy, in proportion to faith; (7) ministry, in ministering; the teacher, in teaching; (8) the exhorter, in exhortation; the giver, in generosity; the leader, in diligence; the compassionate, in cheerfulness.

We all have flaws and limitations. The secret to a meaningful life is to see that our limitations may actually be strengths that we can use. Each of us has a role to play in the kingdom of God, and we need to discover it, not lament over what we think we do not have. Also, note that the water carrier told the sad cracked pot that his contribution was very significant. Not only should we see the strength in our limitations, but we should be ready to point out to others how their ablities and possible contributions to the kingdom might be a lot greater than they first assume.

Rising Floodwaters

An old Cajun lived in a cabin in the bayou of south Louisiana. He "rode out" many storms in his home, and he swore never to leave. Early September one year a hurricane was approaching the wetlands. The forecast was for the water to totally overwhelm the bayou and swamp area where he lived, so people were asked to evacuate. The old Cajun refused to leave. He said to his neighbors, "Cher, I trust in da' Lord to protect. Dat storm, she ain't gonna wash me away. I stay by my home through dis' here flood."

As the waters rose higher with the tidal surge pushed forward by the hurricane, state police drove through the side roads and took the few remaining folk with them to safety shelters on higher ground. They came to the old man, but he refused to go with them. He sat on his porch reading a Bible, and he said, "Cher, I have great faith in da' Lord. He ain't gonna let me down. He will protect. If da' Lord wants me to leave dis' here cabin, He will give me a sign." The state troopers shook their heads and drove on.

The waters rose high, and soon emergency personnel came by in a motor boat. They called to the old man to get in the boat, but he refused. "Da good Lord will protect me, like he protected Noah in the Bible. I trust in da' Lord. If you have da' faith, nothin' is impossible. Da' Lord will tell me when he wants me to leave." The old man refused to wade out to the boat, so they moved on.

The waters rose even higher, and even came into the old man's cabin. He went to the roof of his cabin. A coast guard helicopter flew overhead and dropped him a rope. But he steadfastly refused to climb up the rope, saying, "I just trust in da' Lord, and he will not let me perish. Da' Lord will protect me no matter how bad dis' storm may look. I have faith and I will survive." The helicopter pilot gave up and flew to the next home.

The waters kept rising. The waters rose over the top of the man's cabin, it washed him away, and he drowned.

A little later, after the paperwork at the pearly gates, he was in heaven. While wandering the beautiful streets, he ran into God one day. After exchanging a few pleasantries, the old man felt constrained to ask God about what happened on earth. He said plainly, "Lord I trusted in you. I had great faith in you. I believed dat' you would save me. I thought you would give me a sign if'n you wanted me to leave. But you didn't give me no sign. I died. Now, don't get me wrong! I do really love dis' place, Cher. I really enjoy heaven. But it still sits wrong wid' me that you let me down when I trusted you."

God looked at him and said, "You little twit! You wanted a sign! First, I sent you a car! Then, I sent you a boat! Finally, I sent you a helicopter! You didn't get on any of them. I gave you three signs. You didn't listen to any of them."

I Samuel 3:4-10: (4) Then the Lord called, "Samuel, Samuel!" and he said, "Here I am!" (5) and ran to Eli, and said, "Here I am, for you called me." But he said, "I did not call; lie down again." So he went and lay down. (6) The Lord called again, "Samuel!" Samuel got up and went to Eli, and said, "Here I am, for you called me." But he said, "I did not call, my son; lie down again." (7) Now Samuel did not yet know the Lord, and the word of the Lord had not yet been revealed to him. (8) The Lord called Samuel again, a third time. And he got up and went to Eli, and said, "Here I am, for you called me." Then Eli perceived that the Lord was calling the boy. (9) Therefore Eli said to Samuel, "Go, lie down; and if he calls you, you shall say, 'Speak, Lord, for your servant is listening.'" So Samuel went and lay down in his place. (10) Now the Lord came and stood there, calling as before, "Samuel! Samuel!" And Samuel said, "Speak, for your servant is listening."

Sometimes we are so sure of what we are doing that we don't stop and think that maybe there is another way of doing things, maybe there is another viewpoint, maybe God is calling us to do something other than what we think must be done. We must listen for the voice of God, and sometimes it comes in the advice of other people. Samuel did not know at first that it was God calling him, but when he finally listened, he began a career as a prophetic leader that made him one of the most significant personages in the Old Testament. Always be open to the voice of God in your life.